50 Hikes in™
HELLS CANYON & OREGON'S WALLOWAS

Rhonda Ostertag
and
George Ostertag

THE
MOUNTAINEERS

Published by
The Mountaineers
1001 SW Klickitat Way, Suite 201
Seattle, WA 98134

10 9 8 7
5 4 3 2 1

Published simultaneously in Great Britain by Cordee, 3a DeMontfort Street, Leicester, England, LE1 7HD

Manufactured in the United States of America

Edited by Heidi Robinson
Maps by George Ostertag
All photographs by the authors, unless otherwise noted
Book design and typography by The Mountaineers Books
Book layout by Gray Mouse Graphics

Cover photograph: *Hell's Canyon National Recreation Area, Oregon*
Frontispiece: *Hat Point Trail viewpoint*

Library of Congress Cataloging-in-Publication Data
Ostertag, Rhonda, 1957—
    50 hikes in Hells Canyon & Oregon's Wallowas / Rhonda and George Ostertag.
        p. cm.
    Includes index.
    ISBN 0-89886-521-2
    1. Hiking—Hells Canyon (Idaho and Or.)—Guidebooks. 2. Hiking—Oregon—Wallowa Mountains—Guidebooks. 3. Mountaineering—Hells Canyon (Idaho and Or.)—Guidebooks. 4. Mountaineering—Oregon—Wallowa Mountains—Guidebooks. 5. Backpacking—Hells Canyon (Idaho and Or.)—Guidebooks. 6. Backpacking—Oregon—Wallowa Mountains—Guidebooks. 7. Hells Canyon (Idaho and Or.)—Guidebooks. 8. Wallowa Mountains (Or.)—Guidebooks. I. Ostertag, George, 1957—. II. Title.
GV199.42.H45078 1997
917.95'73—dc21   97-26102
                                                                                      CIP

50 Hikes in™
HELLS CANYON & OREGON'S WALLOWAS

CONTENTS

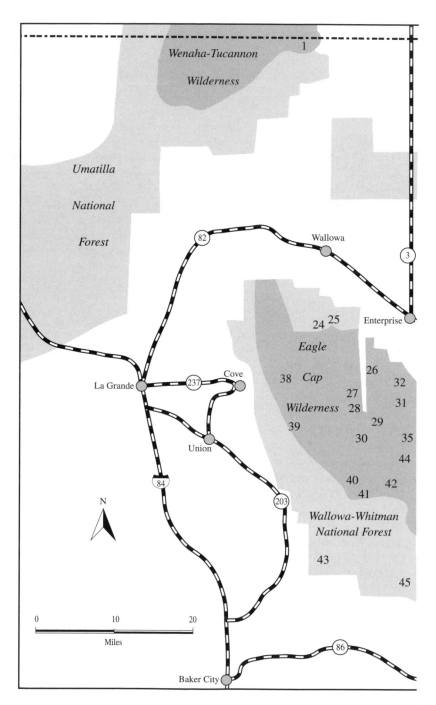

Wenaha-Tucannon

Wilderness

1

Umatilla

National

Forest

82

Wallowa

3

24 25

Enterprise

Eagle

26

38 Cap

32

27

31

Wilderness 28

La Grande

237

Cove

39

29

30

35

Union

44

40

42

41

84

203

Wallowa-Whitman
National Forest

N

43

45

0   10   20
Miles

86

Baker City

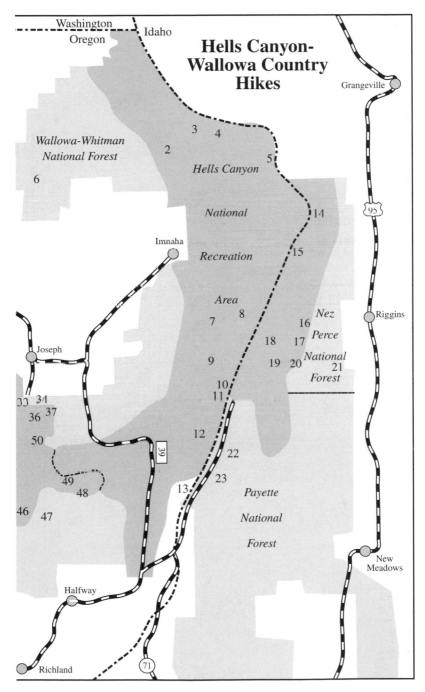

Hells Canyon-
Wallowa Country
Hikes

Washington
Oregon

Idaho

Grangeville

Wallowa-Whitman
National Forest

6

2

3   4

5

Hells Canyon

National

14

95

Recreation

15

Imnaha

Area

8

7

16   Nez
Perce

Riggins

18   17

Joseph

9

19 20 National
21
Forest

10

33 34

11

36 37

50

12

39

22

49

23

48

13

Payette

46   47

National

Forest

Halfway

Richland

71

New
Meadows

INTRODUCTION

The Hells Canyon–Wallowa country of northeastern Oregon and west-central Idaho offers an incredible landscape of contrast and beauty. This premier "wilderness"—whether formally designated by Congress or indisputably so by nature's design—features 1500 miles of trail, ranging from short nature hikes to lengthy river and creek treks to rewarding summit climbs. Passage likewise covers the spectrum: hikers will find comfortable hikes on well-traveled horse trails as well as harsh wilderness campaigns on faint footpaths.

Amid this winning landscape find grassland steppes, arid plateaus, and stony temples juxtaposed with snow-capped peaks, glacial valleys, and alpine lakes. Travel amid stands of stout ponderosa pine, flats of dormant hackberry, and alcoves of elfin whitebark pine and true fir. Wildflowers and waterfalls grace both arid and alpine extremes.

Explore rim and belly of the deepest river-carved canyon in North America—Hells Canyon, the 10-mile-wide rocky cleave of the Snake Wild and Scenic River. Deeper than the Grand Canyon, Hells Canyon boasts an incredible 8,000-foot vertical relief from the top of Idaho's He Devil Peak (elevation 9,393 feet) to the rolling Snake River below (elevation 1,350 feet). Lookout towers atop Oregon's Hat Point and at Heavens Gate and Dry Diggins in Idaho suggest obvious hiker destinations.

The Oregon Wallowas and Hells Canyon's own Seven Devils in Idaho contribute a stirring alpine country, each with its signature geology and high-peak majesty. In the Wallowas, thirty named peaks tower more than 8,000 feet, cradling no fewer than fifty-two named alpine lakes. The Seven Devils Mountains lure with a demonic gallery of 9,000-footers; the lineup is headed by He Devil and includes such hobgoblins as The Ogre, She Devil, and Twin Imps. This range, too, boasts a series of high lakes, with remote Six Lakes Basin expanding the offering southward.

A rich geologic and cultural history permeates the region. Discover clues to the forces that molded and shaped this fascinating terrain: Hells Canyon's origin as a volcanic arc; eons of settling, folding, and faulting; and the erosive powers of water and ice.

Share in the plight and self-reliance of the canyon homesteaders, who battled against heat, poison ivy, rattlesnakes, and isolation. Walk in the footsteps of the Nez Perce, and feel the stirring of gold fever. View the charred overhangs of rock shelters used by Native American hunters more than 7,000 years ago, and decipher the lore of the native people's pictographs.

Wildlife abounds in this vestige. Watch the Snake River roil and splash with a prehistoric sturgeon, spy mountain goat and bighorn sheep atop a rocky precipice, or encounter deer sipping from river or creek. In Hells Canyon, rattlesnake and black widow spider likewise find a niche, underscoring the area's wildness.

The realm tugs at the hiker's wandering spirit, with isolation, the promise of adventure, and the romance and wonder of the wide open

Catherine Creek Cabin

spaces. Only a handful of such untried places still exist in the continental United States.

Geographic remoteness, combined with an unforgiving harshness of both climate and terrain, has kept the Hells Canyon–Wallowa country a raw jewel. But the forces and pressures of a modern-day world lap at the wildland's door—threatening to bring change, and threatening its very identity.

The region's future hangs in question. Can this vital treasure endure?

A POLITICAL HOTBED

The Hells Canyon–Wallowa country represents a critical puzzle piece in the Pacific Northwest: it is the ecological link joining the Northern Rockies, the Blue Mountains, and the Great Basin, and it harbors hallmark qualities of each major ecosystem. It is also the geographic heart of the Columbia River drainage.

Today, this extraordinary place has reached a crossroads. If existing practices and new uses go unchecked, this frontier could be spoiled forever. Most interests agree that the time has come to set cleaner goals for the site's well-being, its growth, and its role in the region's economy. A long-term outlook must replace short-term fixes.

Sorting out the issues, though, has created a contentious political rift, with two major camps facing off. One camp seeks to capitalize on the natural resources of the area, benefiting from timbering, grazing, and a full-blown level of tourism that calls for more paved roads and developed visitor facilities. The other camp advocates preserving the area's wildness and natural beauty, allowing ecological processes to occur free from intervention, and controlling the tourism that already exists. Smaller factions comprise the gray area.

How should this area best be managed? What the nation ultimately answers may determine the quality of this area forever.

THE REGION'S PRESENT MANAGEMENT

The public lands that constitute the Hells Canyon–Wallowa area of northeastern Oregon and western Idaho currently fall under the jurisdiction of the U.S. Forest Service. Core lands include Hells Canyon National Recreation Area (NRA) and Wilderness in both Oregon and Idaho; Wallowa–Whitman National Forest/Eagle Cap Wilderness in Oregon; and portions of Nez Perce and Payette national forests in Idaho.

The greater region spans from the tablelands of the Grande Ronde and Wenaha rivers at the Washington-Oregon border to the Powder River of Oregon to the watershed of the lower Salmon River in Idaho. Nine federally designated Wild and Scenic Rivers thread the Hells Canyon–Wallowa ecosystem: the Snake, Imnaha, Rapid, Wenaha, Grande Ronde, Minam, and Lostine rivers, and Joseph and Eagle creeks.

The federal Wild and Scenic River Act of 1968 sets forth a means for recognizing exceptional national waterways; it describes three river classifications: wild, scenic, and recreational. Wild rivers are the most remote, pristine, and primitive waterways; scenic rivers are unimpounded and largely undeveloped; and recreational rivers have some development in their midst, but continue to offer exceptional recreation. Compatible uses and recreations have been prescribed for each classification.

For designated wilderness areas, the primary management goal is to promote wilderness values. Through current interpretation, some grazing and outfitting align with this goal. A "multiple use" orientation guides the management of the national forest lands that make up the bulk of the region. Historically, this management has advocated motorized tourism, grazing, and timbering, and non-motorized recreation and ecosystems have been given less emphasis.

The act of 1975 that created Hells Canyon National Recreation Area spells out the objectives for the Recreation Area: (1) to provide for public recreation; (2) to protect the free-flowing nature of the rivers; (3) to conserve scenic, wilderness, cultural, and scientific values; (4) to preserve biologically unique features; (5) to protect fish and wildlife habitat; (6) to protect and interpret archaeological sites; (7) to preserve and restore historic sites; and (8) to utilize natural resources such as timber, minerals, and range in a compatible manner.

A BIT OF HISTORY

Hells Canyon was proposed for national park status as early as 1938 and would surely have won approval, but for the pressing business of a world war and the nation's recovery. Protection for the Wallowa Mountain high peaks, what is today Eagle Cap Wilderness, dates to 1940. Added protections and expanded acreage, culminating in the present spread of more than 361,000 acres, make it the largest wilderness area in Oregon.

Designated in 1975 to resolve questions regarding further dam construction on the Snake River, Hells Canyon NRA straddles and protects an impressive stretch of the river. The NRA encompasses more than 652,000 acres. Of that total, 215,000 acres bear wilderness designation.

Hells Canyon Preservation Council (HCPC), a nonprofit organization formed in 1966 that was dedicated to safeguarding the natural values of Hells Canyon, disbanded once NRA protection was ensured; however, as concern grew over the management of the NRA, this watchdog group reorganized.

In 1992, the HCPC along with the National Parks and Conservation Association (NPCA) unveiled a plan calling for the creation of Hells Canyon and the High Wallowas national parks, Snake River Breaks National Recreation Area, and Chief Joseph National Preserve, all of which were to be managed by the National Park Service as Hells Canyon–Chief Joseph National Park and Preserve.

A CRY FOR NATIONAL PARK STATUS

The HCPC's call for the establishment of Hells Canyon–Chief Joseph National Park and Preserve—with the bulk of the land bearing "preserve" status that allows for hunting—has a growing legion of support among businesses, conservation groups, recreationists, and hunters. Already about 65 percent of the proposed park and preserve has won wilderness or national recreation area protection, so the bite out of the public domain and federal coffers would be minimal.

The addition of this park and preserve would fill a glaring void in the national park system, which goes underrepresented in eastern Oregon, eastern Washington, and Idaho. This would be the first national park to recognize the special importance of the volcanic tablelands of the Columbia Plateau; Hells Canyon already figures prominently on nearly every top-ten roster of prospective national parks. After a raft trip through Hells Canyon in 1993, Roger Contor, who has more than 30 years of National Park Service experience, indicated that in his opinion Hells Canyon would outrank all but a few of the existing national parks.

WHO CAN BEST MANAGE THE AREA?

During its watch over the Hells Canyon–Wallowa area, the U.S. Forest Service has fallen under harsh scrutiny. Criticisms leveled at the agency concern its handling of motorized recreation, salvage logging, and grazing allotments; its questionable protection of habitat for wild sheep herds; and its recent development of roads and campgrounds that place cultural sites at risk or mar the river canyon's beauty.

Opponents charge that the U.S. Forest Service has over-emphasized the exploitation of natural resources at a cost to the area's wild vestige and well-being. Opponents further contend that the agency lacks a vision for the area and backs away from decisions that would offend special interest groups. Hells Canyon Preservation Council, National Parks and Conservation Association, many Native Americans, and several environmental groups comprise the forces aligned against the U.S. Forest Service.

This group holds that the National Park Service (NPS) should be the rightful management agency, and strongly recommends national park and preserve status for the area. The group contends that the NPS, which has held the charge of protecting and promoting our national treasures since inception, can best guide the use and development of this area.

Proponents of the Forest Service include ranchers, jet boaters, certain tourist groups, several local businesses, and many within the surrounding communities. These supporters contend that the agency has done a good job managing traditional enterprises while keeping to the terms of the NRA act. They prefer an "as-is" management and hold suspect the rules and regulations (i.e. restrictions) that accompany a national park.

Funding, too, is at issue. Would the NPS be able to provide the necessary oversight for this vast, remote property? If approved, Hells Canyon–Chief Joseph National Park and Preserve would rank among the largest national parks in the contiguous forty-eight states.

Current shortfalls in federal funding have already hurt the Forest Service in its management, denying funds for recreation, enforcement of regulations, trail maintenance, facilities and road upkeep, restoration, and development. The Forest Service has even justified past logging levels as a means to finance recreation programs.

As an interim measure, the HCPC has offered to work with the Forest Service in promoting ecosystem restoration and showcasing imperiled wildlife, and has even offered to help secure funding. So far the offer has gone unaddressed.

Regardless of who takes the reins for this area, under whatever protective designation, two points are clear: (1) Some change is inevitable, and (2) strong contingents of concerned citizens will be watching.

CONTROVERSIES

Jet boating versus river floating. The issue of jet boaters versus river floaters represents one of the most contentious battles in Hells Canyon. Emotions run high, and at times have been accompanied by slurs and even gunshots.

Since the 1970s, the total jet boat traffic in Hells Canyon has increased fivefold, despite a legal requirement that the U.S. Forest Service control the number of motorized boats. The Forest Service endorses a shared-use river policy with some suggested river-safety rules. In the NRA, number restrictions have always applied to floaters while jet boaters are only now facing some curtailment of use and number.

With increased boating numbers and an overall lack of cooperation regarding right-of-way, speed, and common courtesy, a stronger management hand is in the offing. A balance must be struck that satisfies the safety and economic concerns while addressing the overriding concern of ensuring the long-term integrity of the Snake Wild and Scenic River.

Advocates for jet boating claim they have a historical precedence in the canyon that is protected under the NRA act of 1975. They further point to the Snake River as being one of the last wild rivers open to them for running. As a service, jet boat operations do introduce the river canyon to parties who would otherwise not have the stamina or physical ability to see it. They also serve visitors with limited time.

The chief environmental repercussions from these boats are noise pollution heard from river to rim, fumes, and bank erosion. While the boats do not appear to spook wildlife, they could affect the animals' health and well-being in unseen ways.

On the basis of economics, commercial jet boat operators have long objected to proposed management plans that restrict user numbers or impose river schedules. Commercial operators argued that past prescribed schedules were confusing and difficult to adhere to and enforce, and expressed worry that restrictions would complicate their booking and filling of charters.

Conversely, number restrictions do apply to river floaters and the inequity is sorely felt: rafters or kayakers wishing to make a private float trip between Memorial Day weekend and September 15 must request reservations by submitting their applications the preceding December or January.

With few river bars or flats being suitable for campsites and with most float trips lasting more than a day's time, such number restrictions help protect the canyon from overuse. While rafters can accept this logic, they cannot condone allowing unlimited jet boats, which also negatively impact the river.

Commercial floaters, like the commercial jet boat operators, make a living guiding river tours and do not escape the economic pinch of restrictions. For the most part, float trips are more labor- and time-intensive and accommodate fewer numbers, and often trip quality is adversely affected by the noise, wakes, and danger posed by jet boats.

The time has come to put this controversy to rest. The Forest Service must set and keep limits, prescribe a river etiquette, and define appropriate practices for both groups of river users. The agency must also separate river users for their own safety.

This separation may be made according to the days of the week or by river segment. Key to the debate is the 31.5-mile "wild" section of the Snake River. Does it become the exclusive domain of river floaters, with the remaining river set aside for jet boats? Solutions do not come without anger, but the river requires order.

Domestic sheep versus bighorn sheep. The grazing of domestic sheep has been an ongoing practice in Hells Canyon since the 1800s, and is a sanctioned enterprise under the NRA act of 1975. While native bighorn sheep disappeared from the canyon in the 1940s, eradicated by over-hunting and domestic sheep diseases, Rocky Mountain bighorns have since been reintroduced. Both wild and domestic sheep herds now roam the canyon.

A similar situation exists in the Wallowa Mountains, where reintroduced herds of both bighorn sheep and mountain goats range in proximity with domestic sheep. The closeness has proven deadly to the wild sheep herds, which have lost more than half their numbers to pneumonia.

Biologists now generally concur that the causal Pasteurella pathogens are transmitted directly from the domestic sheep, which seem to carry immunity, to the wild sheep, which do not. Studies with inoculation have proven ineffective.

The present resolution seems to be one of "either-or": either the agency discontinues the grazing of domestic sheep, or it halts the reintroduction of wild sheep. In 1996, Supervisor Robert Richmond moved for the temporary removal of domestic sheep herds from most of Hells Canyon National Recreation Area, with no action taken in the Eagle Cap Area of the Wallowas.

Local sheep ranchers view such action as a threat to their livelihood, tradition, and rural culture, but hunters and naturalists welcome the move.

Cattle grazing versus grassland integrity and stream purity. Three-quarters of the NRA, portions of Eagle Cap Wilderness, and tracts of national forest allow for grazing, with the range being vital to the local stockmen who work their herds from low to high range. Generations of ranchers have used these lands and rely on them for their livelihood, and ranching is clearly part of the region's character and heritage.

Yet grasses cropped too short or badly trampled may not recover, resulting in the loss of native grasses. These degraded grasslands, in turn, steal from wildlife habitat. The thin-soiled terraces of Hells Canyon prove particularly vulnerable. When uncontrolled, cattle likewise trample stream banks and spoil pristine waters with their waste. Subsequently, the silty streams harm fish habitat and deprive anadromous fish of the necessary spawning gravel.

Most ranchers would prefer that the region's range management go unchanged, while some environmental groups would advocate a swift and total removal of all cattle within NRA and wilderness lands. Hells Canyon Preservation Council calls for a gradual

Grazing at Pittsburg Landing

draw down of grazing. The policy they advocate would allow for traditional grazing by current landowners and permittees, but as allotments are given up, they would be retired from offer.

The HCPC further advocates environmental measurements that would ensure that the long-term quality of both grassland and streams be applied to range practices. The council recommends that the presently unused allotments remain ungrazed to allow for recovery and to provide a standard by which to measure the grazed lands. If grasslands cannot recover and improve with cattle on them, then the cattle should be removed. Similarly, if riparian environments (wetlands, springs, streams, and seeps) suffer degradation, grazing should be prohibited.

While such mitigating measures come with a degree of inconvenience and cost to land-users, the end result of enduring, high-quality range benefits all: ranchers, wildlife, naturalists, and recreationists.

Dams versus a wild river, dams versus salmon. Although the NRA act of 1975 squelched any prospect of building future dams within Hells Canyon, it did not consider the question of preserving the existing dams up and downstream on the Snake River.

With the undeniable, fateful decline in salmon runs, preservation groups have come to view at least the two upper Snake River dams with an eye toward destruction. These dams block salmon migration, sealing off passage to seven major upstream river systems. Moreover, they prevent the natural floods that used to carry the fingerlings safely to sea.

Hells Canyon Dam

With an ineffective fish ladder or no ladder at all, the two upper dams pose an insurmountable challenge to a fish species struggling for survival. Artificial means to facilitate migration have failed miserably. At Brownlee Dam, a failed netting of migrating juveniles resulted in the majority of the salmon dying in the reservoir. A fish trap malfunction at Oxbow Dam killed 4,000 Chinook in a stagnant pool. To compound the problem, Hells Canyon Dam (above the wild river) blocks sediments, which results in the loss of natural beaches and adversely affects the river's nitrogen level.

Unfortunately, existing salmon numbers are too low to allow for much more experimentation. Traditional salmon habitats and passageways must be remedied and restored. Even the U.S. Army Corps of Engineers concedes that breaching all four federal dams on the lower Snake River (Ice Harbor, Lower Monumental, Little Goose, and Lower Granite dams) deserves study.

The salmon, besides being a critical food source and vital commercial and recreational enterprise, are also an emblem of the Northwest and part of Native American culture. The price tag for removing or breaching the dams, though, runs high and its effect on the economy would only begin with an increase in electricity rates; however, even this action may not be enough to save the region's salmon.

Timbering versus park protection. Historically, logging has been a driving enterprise in the region, along with agriculture. Should park protection be granted to the Hells Canyon–Wallowa area, boundaries drawn beyond the Eagle Cap and Hells Canyon wilderness areas would deprive the region of a portion of its logging base.

While some shock waves would ripple through the surrounding communities, the towns have demonstrated a past resilience. Wallowa County dealt with the closure of two of its three mills without major long-term consequence to the overall economy. Still, individuals did lose jobs.

The logging base removed by the proposed national park and preserve would be the least accessible, least productive in the area. Additionally, logging no longer represents the stable employment that it did in the past. The role of logging is changing as the nation comes to value habitat over board feet, to question just how real sustainable yield is, and to weigh biological values against the economic value (and cost) of clear-cutting.

Some area businesses view the establishment of the park and preserve as a way to counter the downsizing of the timber industry. They believe that accompanying service jobs will be forthcoming, sustaining, and compatible with the traditional lifestyles of the region. The HCPC, however, does not concur with the belief that timber jobs should be replaced with tourism. The council believes that tourism already exists and that it is a factor to be managed, not promoted.

Hikers versus packers. Smaller battles periodically erupt in the Hells Canyon–Wallowa area, particularly in the alpine backcountry. Hiking purists protest the use of livestock, complaining of trail and habitat degradation, manure and increased flies, oversized camps, and large pack party numbers.

Packer, Lostine River Trail

Cooperative measures taken by the Forest Service and area packers have mitigated most of these arguments. Packers have strict rules regarding party size, how and where they may pitch camp, and feeding, tethering, watering, and cleaning up after stock. If everyone heeds the rules and strives toward no-trace travel, use of the backcountry should continue to accommodate both groups. Hikers should also remember that packers and area horse clubs provide the vital volunteer service of building and repairing bridges and clearing and opening trails.

Commercialism versus natural wild. Will this area become another over-used Yellowstone? Over-commercialized Yosemite? Or will it be allowed to prosper as a relatively wild park such as North Cascades in Washington State?

These questions strongly affect the immediate communities and their family values. Some in the local chambers of commerce view a fully accessible, developed national park as a favorable end that would bring jobs and stimulate the area's economy. Others view development with suspicion, believing that family-run hotels and eateries would be pushed out by commercial chains and that there would be a loss of the rural quiet and natural splendor.

The question at the fore of this controversy should be "How much access can this delicate environment endure?" Without care, what once was an unvisited backcountry runs the risk of becoming besieged by pavement, tour buses, carloads of vacationing travelers, and jet boats. It would be a shame to lose this raw vestige. The question of development should be addressed reverently and slowly, as once in place it will be impossible to remove or reverse.

WHEN YOU VISIT

Weather. Lower elevations offer nearly year-round travel, while alpine reaches hold but two-season hiking in summer and fall. Some hiking trails double as winter cross-country ski and snowshoe trails.

With 8,000 feet of vertical relief in Hells Canyon, expect a wide range of weather and temperature variation between seasons and between elevations. The lower canyon experiences relatively mild winters with snows claiming the rims and high country. Summers find canyon-bottom temperatures in excess of 100 degrees Fahrenheit; loftier reaches can be 20 degrees or more cooler. Wind and exposure can also affect the weather profile.

Typically most trails within Eagle Cap and Seven Devils open by July 4 and remain open through October. Summer highs can reach 90 degrees Fahrenheit, and lows may be as cool as 40 degrees. Afternoon thunderstorms and unseasonal snowstorms do hit the area. The lake regions endure short, tormenting mosquito and biting fly seasons. Come armed with repellent.

Habitat. This perpendicular terrain boasts a variety of habitats: bald outcrops and promontories; grand waterfalls; clear-coursing rivers and streams; high mountain lakes; vegetated draws; low-, mid-, and high-elevation forests; wildflower meadows; grassland terraces; and desert plains.

Cultural history. Stumble upon the paths of Chief Joseph and early-day explorer Benjamin Bonneville. Find evidence of early native peoples dating back more than 7,000 years. Rock shelters, evidence of pit houses, and petroglyphs and pictographs provide clues.

In the 1860s, mining—first placer, then hard rock—came onto the scene. Discover claims and artifacts along the Imnaha River in Hells Canyon and near Cornucopia in the Wallowas. Along the Snake River, Chinese miners erected semi-subterranean stone houses.

In 1910, some 100 families homesteaded along a 62-mile stretch of the Snake River between Battle Creek and the Imnaha River. By 1918, only a small number remained as the canyon exacted its grueling toll. Old cabins and outbuildings dot the landscape recalling the era. Active ranches still exist along the Imnaha and Snake rivers.

All cultural sites and artifacts are protected under law; admire but do not disturb.

Land ownership. This book concentrates on public land offerings, although some private parcels may lie along or border routes. Wherever possible, hikers will be alerted to these areas. When traveling right-of-ways across private property, hikers assume responsibility for their own well-being and enter an unspoken pact to heed posted rules and respect private property and privacy. Keep to the trail, leave gates as they were found, and police your own actions as well as the actions of the less thoughtful who may have passed before you.

Road access. The shortest paved loop encircling Hells Canyon NRA measures 400 miles; no roads cross the canyon within the NRA, and few roads explore the canyon. Only three roads access the Snake River: at Dug Bar, at Pittsburg Landing, and at Hells Canyon Creek.

To date, 75 percent of the canyon remains roadless. Roads that do probe the canyon typically require four-wheel drive and high clearance for the steep, rough terrain. The USFS has upgraded some key roads with gravel or paved surfaces, providing visitor access to critical viewpoints and to new camp facilities.

The core of the Wallowa Mountains likewise remains inaccessible. While numerous forest roads web the periphery, not all are suitable for passenger vehicles. Visitors still need to exit the car and walk to truly see the area.

Horse and llama pack stations, jet boats, and a small airplane charter out of Enterprise, Oregon to Minam Lodge offer alternate means of access.

With services limited and far between, keep vehicles in good repair, check tires for good rubber and tread, top gas tanks when the opportunity presents itself, and keep maps handy. Carry emergency gear: spare tire, jumper cables, extra belts, water for the radiator, and perhaps a saw for tree removal. Also carry emergency overnight items: food, drinking water, warm clothes, blankets, flashlight, and first-aid kit.

Before starting any Hells Canyon–Wallowa outing, it is advisable to contact the Wallowa Mountains Visitor Center (1 mile west of Enterprise, Oregon), the Hells Canyon office in Riggins, Idaho, or the managing district Forest Service office for current road (and trail) information. Even major roads are vulnerable to damage from flooding, mudslide, and erosion. A simple phone call can save you needless road miles and put you on the trail faster.

Trail markings and condition. Most maintained trails have standard cut beds, requiring only junction signs to clarify crossroads. A few trails, however, consist of faintly worn or rapidly overgrown paths that require additional guidance. Markings typically come in the form of shaved-bark blazes, cairns, or trail stakes. In some cases, hikers must scout out the trail. Look for log cuts and removed lower branches that hint at previous trail maintenance.

In the alpine outback of the Wallowas and Seven Devils, travel typically follows well-defined and well-maintained horse trails. Bridges may span the more difficult waters, but many streams still require fording. Come prepared. High-use trails receive annual maintenance; all others fall under a rotation system.

In the grasslands and canyon drainages of Hells Canyon, expect more difficult conditions. Steep terrain and light use contribute to faint footpaths that can easily be confused with livestock or wildlife paths. In moist draws, the vegetation grows rampant, quickly overtaking even the recently brushed out trails. Bushwhacking through poison ivy, nettles, and tall grasses can wear out hikers; adjust hiking times accordingly. Be alert while traveling to avoid straying off course.

Summit Ridge Trailhead cairn

Trail Park Passes. Under this new program to generate funds for trail maintenance and improvements, the U.S. Forest Service will require trail users to obtain a daily or annual trail park pass before coming to and parking within 0.25 mile of specified trailheads. While still in the experimental stage, this pass will be sold much as the Sno-park passes currently are: purchase passes at USFS offices or at various retail outlets. Annual passes offer hikers flexibility in trip planning and are welcomed at trailheads in both Oregon and Washington.

Wilderness permits and regulations. For wilderness travel in Hells Canyon and Eagle Cap, hikers must secure a free permit at the trailhead self-register station or from an area U.S. Forest Service office. Permits for Eagle Cap Wilderness are required from May 24 through November 30.

There are no restrictions on hiker numbers at present. Complete the permit and have it in your possession while hiking. These permits allow for the tracking of visitor use, number, and activity, and for determining and mitigating over use.

Despite the remote location, this vulnerable wild requires special protection. Rules regarding access, group size, and acceptable camp and sanitation parameters may change over time to ensure that protection. Acquaint yourself with the current rules and adhere to them.

The present maximum group size consists of eight people and sixteen stock (eight riders, eight mounts, and eight pack animals), with no exceptions allowed. In the taxed, highly sensitive Wallowa Lakes Basin, the party size restriction is six people, twelve stock. Organized groups, including Boy Scouts or family gatherings that exceed six or eight people, must go elsewhere or disperse to travel in smaller bands to alternate sites.

Locate campsites and campfires no closer than 200 feet to any lake, spring, stream, or wetland. Campfires may not be built within 0.25 mile of any of the following Eagle Cap high lakes: Bear (Bear Creek area), Chimney, Eagle, Glacier, Laverty, Mirror, Moccasin, Steamboat, Sunshine, Swamp, and Upper. Practice no-trace travel at all times.

Volunteers. As the U.S. Forest Service experiences a declining recreational budget, devoted, energetic volunteers help bridge the gap for trail building, maintenance, and improvement. At the forefront are area horse clubs and environmental organizations, but the importance of individuals cannot be overlooked.

Thanks to volunteers, unsafe bridges have been dismantled, new bridges built, natural areas have been rehabilitated, and trails have been maintained and built. Even still, some trails may go uncleared and repairs unmade. All hikers should support these dedicated volunteers and actively join in the effort themselves.

USING THIS BOOK

This book invites hikers to visit the Hells Canyon–Wallowa area—to discover its majesty, to discover what is at stake.

With hundreds of hikes from which to choose, we focused our attention on the trails that showcase the area, present the spectrum of offering, represent a range of difficulty, and may be accessed by reliable roads. Most of the selected trailheads may be accessed by passenger vehicles; exceptions are clearly noted. Before visiting any of the trails, hikers should phone to be sure the roads and trails are open. Fires, avalanches, floods, blow-downs, and mudslides can alter conditions and consequently plans.

Generally, we tried to select trails that lend themselves to day hikes, but virtually all of the trails are equally suited to backpackers because any hike may be shortened or lengthened. An intricate web of backcountry travel awaits.

We have structured the book to aid in the trail selection process. First, we have grouped the trails into four geographical areas to ease page-flipping comparisons. Second, each write-up is preceded by a summary table of trail information: distance, high point, elevation change, an information source, and maps are all identified. Turn to the appendix for the complete address and phone for each named source.

Within the text you will find an introduction to the area, detailed directions to the trailhead, and a description of the trail's progress that draws attention to special features as well as to obstacles and potentially confusing junctions. Mentions of habitat changes, seasonal surprises, sidelights, and discoveries flesh out the tour. Where appropriate, we have mentioned flaws and disappointments. Within the text, references to trail numbers represent the management numbers used on agency maps and materials.

The maps included within the text are not intended to replace the more detailed agency maps, road maps, state atlases, or topographic maps, but they do indicate the lay of the trail and its main features in order to help readers visualize the tour.

AN EXPLANATION OF SUMMARY TABLE TERMS

Distance measures for the trails represent pedometer readings. Backpacking excursions—sometimes dictated by distance, sometimes by attraction—are left to the hiker's judgment.

We deliberately excluded estimated hiking times, as personal health and physical condition, party size, overall appeal of the trail, weather, and trail conditions all influence travel time. To best estimate hiking time, consider your personal capabilities and hiking style, and judge the time based on distance, elevation change, and what you glean from the text.

GLOSSARY

Car-shuttle hikes. These are linear routes that allow for one-way travel with either a drop-off and pick-up arrangement or the spotting of a second vehicle at the trail's end. If no transportation is at the trail's end, you must hike back out.

Corduroy. This side-by-side alignment of logs, boards, or branches provides a dry passage over soggy trail segments or delicate meadow sites.

Improved-surface roads. These roads are unpaved with gravel or compacted dirt surfaces. They may be rutted and washboard, but are generally all-weather routes when clear of snow.

Jeep trails. These two-track routes typically serve foot and horse travelers; most are no longer drivable.

Switchback. This trail design feature is frequently used on steep slopes, where the trail hooks back on itself for a gentler uphill or downhill grade, advancing via zigzags.

OUTDOOR PRIMER

Whether wilderness trekking brings about a revitalizing experience or becomes an ordeal depends largely on preparation. Nature is not without inherent risks and discomforts, but learning to anticipate them and to mitigate the difficulties smooths the way to great outdoor fun.

PREPARATION

Ten Essentials. Outdoor experts have assembled a list of "Ten Essentials" that are the cornerstone of safe backcountry travel. They are (1) extra food, (2) extra clothing, (3) sunglasses, (4) knife, (5) candle or chemical fuel to ignite wet wood, (6) dry matches, (7) first-aid kit and manual, (8) flashlight with extra bulb and batteries, (9) maps for the trip, and (10) compass.

Dress. The amount and types of clothing worn and carried on a hike depend on the length of the outing, weather conditions, and personal comfort needs. Layering is key to comfort. Select items that can serve more than one purpose: a long-sleeve shirt may be layered for warmth, lends sun protection, and hinders mosquitos; a lightweight raincoat can double as a windbreaker.

Choose wool or a good synthetic fleece for cold, damp, or changeable weather conditions; these fabrics retain heat even when wet. Choose cotton for dry summer days. For their weight, hats are invaluable for shielding the eyes, face, and top of the head, and for preserving body heat. A full suit of raingear likewise earns its way, as wet clothes lose 90 percent of their insulating value.

Footgear. While sneakers may be passable for nature walks, wear boots for comfort and protection on long hikes or on uneven terrain. Sock layering, with a light undersock worn next to the foot and a wool sock worn atop, helps prevent rubbing, cushions the sole, and allows for the absorption of perspiration. Avoid socks with a high cotton content as they are cold when wet and slow to dry.

Food. Pack plenty as hiking demands a lot of energy. Maximize the energy value of food for the weight, particularly when backpacking, and choose foods that will not spoil, bruise, or break apart in the pack. Food fends off fatigue, which is a major contributor to accidents on the trail.

Equipment. The quantity and variety of equipment depend on the length and nature of the hike and on the season, but a good pack for transporting gear is essential. A day pack with padded straps, a reinforced bottom, and side pockets for water bottles works for most short outings. For overnight outings, select a backpack that has a good frame and balance and supports the weight without taxing the hips, shoulders, or neck.

As backpacks represent a major investment, newcomers should first try renting one. Packs cannot be accurately evaluated in the store with only a few sandbags for weight. A trail test delivers a better comfort reading, plus it demonstrates how well the unit packs with one's personal gear. Most good backpacking stores with a rental program will deduct the charge of one rental from the purchase price of a new pack; ask the manager.

Map and Compass. All hikers should become familiar with maps and know how to read them in conjunction with a compass. Maps provide orientation to an area, suggest alternate routes, and aid in planning and trip preparation.

Become familiar with the United States Geological Survey (USGS) topographic maps. While most of these quadrangle maps are dated, they still provide information about the steepness and flatness of the terrain, whether a site is treed or open, waterways, and the works of man. The USGS offers two sizes: the 7.5-minute and 15-minute series.

For the Wallowa Mountains, the privately produced Imus Geographics map offers USGS detail with all of the official trails to date clearly indicated. Marked trailheads and incremental mileages further aid hikers.

Remember that true north does not equal magnetic north. For this region, the declination is about 17 degrees east; search map borders for the exact declination.

TAKING TO THE TRAILS

Pacing yourself. Adopt a steady, comfortable hiking rhythm, take in the surroundings, and schedule short rests at regular intervals to guard against exhaustion.

Crossing streams. Cross at the widest part of a watercourse, where the current is slower and the water more shallow. Sandy bottoms suggest a barefoot crossing; fast, cold waters and rocky bottoms require the surer footing of camp shoes (if they fit snugly and have a good sole for traction) or hiking boots.

Before commencing a boot-clad wade, shed socks. Once across, you will still have a dry sock layer to help protect and warm your feet in the wet boots; this is where wool socks show their thermal value. The discomfort of hiking in wet boots is minor compared to the alternative dunking. For frequent stream crossings or for hiking streambeds, lightweight sneakers earn their portage.

Hiking cross-country. For safe cross-country travel, one must have a good map, compass, survival skills, and solid common sense. Steep terrain, heavy brush, and downfalls physically and mentally tax hikers, which increases the potential for injury. Of all hiking, this type should not be attempted alone. Even know-how and preparation cannot fully overcome the unpredictability of nature and human fallibility.

Hiking through burn habitats. Lightning-caused fires are part of this region's wild character. Such fires are key to the life-cycle of the forest: they cull diseased and dying trees, open stands, and renew native vegetation. In wilderness areas, the Forest Service typically allows natural fires to burn while suppressing human-caused ones. When hiking

Rapid River fire area

through a burn, be alert for dangling overhead branches and the possibility of falling trees. Downfalls may result in steeple chase travel, tiring hikers. Generally, it is advisable to select a camp outside the burn area. Carry plenty of water.

Hiking with children. When hiking with young children. choose simple destinations and do not insist on reaching any particular site. Allow for the difference in attention span and energy level. Enjoy the passing, and share and encourage children's natural curiosity, but come prepared for sun, mosquitos, and poison ivy. Discuss what to do should you become separated; even small children should carry some essential items: a sweater, water jug, and food.

Hiking shared-use trails. Unless otherwise posted, the rule of right-of-way has mountain bikers yielding to both hikers and horseback riders, and hikers, in turn, yielding to horses. Horses may spook and put riders at risk, so yielding means stopping, with all party members stepping to the same side of the trail. Avoid sudden movements, but feel free to speak in normal tones. Voices reassure horses that you are indeed human and not alien creatures.

A WILDERNESS ETHIC

Trails. Keep to the path. Shortcutting, skirting puddles, and walking two abreast all contribute to erosion and the degradation of trails. Report any damage.

Permits and Registration. Secure hiking permits for the wilderness areas at the appropriate U.S. Forest Service ranger station or at a self-registration box at the trailhead. Permits help land agencies measure, monitor, and manage the trails and help minimize over-use.

Pets. Owners should strictly adhere to posted rules for pets. Controlling your animal on a leash is not just a courtesy reserved for times when other hikers are present; it is a responsibility to protect wildlife and ground cover at all times. Know that dogs represent a threat to

Wilderness registration station

horses and may create problems with bears.

Camping. No-trace camping should be everyone's goal. Select an established campsite and do not alter the ground cover, bring in logs for benches, bang nails into trees, or dig drainage channels around the tent. The clues that a hiker passed this way should be minimal.

Where no pre-established campsite exists, select a site at least 200 feet from water sources and well-removed from any trail. Avoid delicate meadow and alpine environments, and do not degrade lakeshore, waterfall, overlook, or other prized sites with a camp.

Reduce comforts (as opposed to necessities), and carry a backpacker's stove for cooking. When a campfire is unavoidable, keep it small and build only in existing fire rings and only where safe and legally permitted. Snags and live trees should never be cut. Fully extinguish all fires by thoroughly mixing water or soil with the ash. Touch the ash to be sure it is out.

Smoking. Where fires present extreme danger or where habitats are particularly sensitive, smoking may be prohibited; heed regulations. Where and when it is allowed, never smoke while hiking. Instead, stop, clear an area to the mineral soil, smoke the cigarette, crush it and all of the ash out, and pack out any cigarette butts.

Sanitation. Always use established backcountry toilets when available. When they are not, select a site well away from the trail and at least 300 feet from any water body for human waste disposal. There dig a "cat hole" 8 inches deep in which to bury the waste. This biologically active layer of soil holds organisms that can quickly decompose organic matter. If the ground resists a trowel, dig as deep as possible and cover well with gravel, bark, and leaves. Cat holes are generally unnecessary for urination.

Pack out soiled tissue using a zip-seal plastic bag. Women's sanitary products should likewise be packed out.

Litter. "Pack it in, pack it out." This includes aluminum foil, cans, orange peels, peanut shells, cigarette butts, and disposable diapers. It takes nature six months to reclaim an orange peel, and a filter-tip cigarette butt takes ten to twelve years. Disposable diapers have become

Campsite along Seven Devils Trail

an incredible nuisance and a contaminant in the wild; burying them is not a solution.

Washing. Washing of self or dishes should be done well away from lakes and streams. Carry wash water to a rocky site and use biodegradable suds sparingly. Despite their benefits and ecological-sounding name, these soaps still present a threat to water.

SAFETY

Water. Water is the preferred trail refreshment; carry a safe quantity at all times as wilderness sources may dry up or become fouled. Know that caffeine and alcohol are diuretics that dehydrate and weaken hikers' systems.

When taken from wilderness sources, drinking water and any water used to wash food or eating utensils should be treated. *Giardia lamblia*, a waterborne protozoan that causes stomach and intestinal discomfort, lives in even the most remote, clear streams. The incubation period ranges from 6 to 15 days; symptoms may include nausea, abdominal distress, lethargy, diarrhea, and weight loss.

Sophisticated water purification systems that strain out harmful organisms and remove debris offer the most convenient, and perhaps the most complete, solution to the problem and are readily available at

Pumping water on Eagle Creek

most outdoor stores. Without such a system, bring the water to a full, rolling boil for at least five minutes. While both time consuming and requiring the portage of a backpacker stove and extra fuel, it is the only other way to insure that the water is safe. Iodine tablets offer less protection against contaminated water, no protection against *Giardia*, and are unsafe for pregnant women.

Getting lost. Prior to departure, notify a responsible party of your intended destination, route, and time of return. Then keep to your itinerary and notify the person upon your return.

If lost, sit down and try to think calmly. No immediate danger exists, as long as one has packed properly and followed the notification procedure. If hiking with a group, stay together. Short outward searches for the trail, returning to an agreed-upon, marked location if unsuccessful, are generally considered safe. If near a watercourse, following it downstream typically leads to a place of habitation or a roadway where help may be sought. Aimless wandering is a mistake.

Blowing a whistle or making loud noises in sets of three may summon help. (Combinations of three are universally recognized as distress signals.) If late in the day, prepare for night and try to conserve energy. Unless one has good cross-country navigational skills, efforts are best spent conserving energy and aiding rescuers by staying put and hanging out brightly colored clothing.

Hypothermia. The number one killer of outdoor recreationists is hypothermia, a dramatic cooling of the body when heat loss surpasses body-heat generation.

Cold, wet, and windy weather command respect. Attending to the Ten Essentials, eating properly, avoiding fatigue, and being alert to the symptoms of sluggishness, clumsiness, and incoherence among party members are the best protection. Should a party member display such symptoms, stop and get that person dry and warm. Shared body heat and hot fluids help in mild hypothermia cases. The severely hypothermic victim should be rushed to a proper medical facility.

Most hypothermia cases develop in air temperatures between 30 and 50 degrees Fahrenheit, and affected individuals may deny having any problem at all. Let the symptoms be your guide to action.

Heat exhaustion. Strenuous exercise combined with summer sun can lead to heat exhaustion, an over-taxation of the body's heat regulatory system, including a complete shut-down of sweating. Wearing a hat, drinking plenty of water, eating properly (including salty snacks), and avoiding fatigue are safeguards. Watch for symptoms of hot, red skin, restricted pupils, and high body temperature.

Dehydration. Humans require a minimum of 2 quarts of water per day and up to 4 quarts while hiking. Heat and strenuous activity at high elevations increase the need for water. Water deprivation weakens hikers both physically and mentally, can cause abdominal and urinary distress, and can lead to shock. Symptoms include pale, moist skin, dilated pupils, nausea, and disorientation.

Altitude sickness. Hikers need to allow their bodies to acclimate to great or rapid altitude changes. As a rule of thumb, avoid ascents of more than 2,000 feet a day between 5,000 and 10,000 vertical feet.

Poison ivy and poison oak. The best way to avoid contact with these and other skin-irritating plants is to learn what they look like and in what environments they grow. Consult a good plant identification book. Vaccines and creams have yet to completely conquer these irritating plant oils, but some products on the market claim to reduce the chance for irritation, with pre- or post-contact applications. If you suspect you have come in contact with one of these plants, rinse off as soon as possible and avoid scratching as it spreads the oils.

Ticks, stings, and bites. As with poisonous plants, the best defense is knowledge. Learn about the habits and habitats of rattlesnakes, poisonous spiders, bees, wasps, ticks, and other "menaces" and how to deal with the injuries they may cause. Also be aware of any personal allergies and sensitivities you or a party member might have.

Rattlesnakes are typically most active May through September, but be alert for them almost any time. Watch the trail ahead, look where you intend to sit or place your hand, and be careful when stepping over logs or rocks. If bitten, remain calm and constrict the blood flow both above and below the bite. Do not apply tourniquets, which may cause more damage than they prevent, and never attempt the "cut and suck" method of field treatment. Avoid exertion, but get to a medical facility as soon as possible.

Statistics show that very few victims of rattlesnake bites are injected with sufficient venom to bring on severe injury or death. Rattlesnakes rely on venom to feed and cannot rapidly replace lost venom, so it is against their best interest to strike humans.

Black widow spiders dwell in the lower elevations of Hells Canyon. Watch for them in pit toilets, near old outbuildings, and under rocks or logs.

Lyme disease, transmitted by the tiny deer tick, has yet to become the concern that it is in the East, but ticks still pose potential threats. During tick season (spring and summer), hikers may wish to don light-colored long pants and long-sleeved shirts, keeping layers tucked into one another. Dressing in this manner makes ticks easier to spot and will keep them outside of garments. Make frequent checks for the unwanted hitchhiker. When at home, shower, search skin surfaces thoroughly, and launder hiking clothes promptly.

Should a tick bite and become lodged in the skin, remove it by drawing evenly on the body, disinfect the site with alcohol, and monitor the bite area over the following few weeks. If any symptoms of illness are experienced, consult a physician immediately.

Bears. When traveling in bear country, use common sense. Do not store food near camp, and especially not in the tent. If clothes pick up cooking smells, suspend them along with the food from an isolated overhanging branch, using counterbalanced weights. Sweet-smelling creams or lotions should be avoided.

Avoid coming between mother and cub, make noise so as not to startle a bear, and keep your distance.

Hunting. While most public lands open to hunters do not prohibit hiking during hunting season and few have any record of conflict, we would still advise fall hikers to point their boots toward lands and trails where hunting is not allowed. If you hike where hunting occurs, wear bright orange clothing and keep to the trail.

Trailhead Precautions. Unattended hiker vehicles are vulnerable to break-ins, but the following steps can minimize the risk:

- Whenever possible, park away from the trailhead at a nearby campground or other facility.
- Do not leave valuables. Place keys and wallet in a button-secured pocket or a secure compartment in the pack where they will not be disturbed until your return.
- Do not leave any visible invitations: stash everything in the trunk, and be sure any exposed item advertises that it has no value.
- Be suspicious of loiterers and do not volunteer the details of your outing.
- Be cautious about the information you supply at the trailhead register.

Backcountry travel includes unavoidable risks that every traveler assumes and must be aware of and respect. The fact that a trail or an area is described in this book is not a representation that it will be safe for you. While this book attempts to alert users to safe methods and warn of potential dangers, it is limited: time, nature, use, and abuse can quickly alter the face of a trail. Let independent judgment and common sense be your guide.

For more detailed information about outdoor preparedness, consult a good instructional book or enroll in a class on outdoor etiquette, procedures, and safety. Even the outdoor veteran can benefit from a refresher.

ACKNOWLEDGMENTS

We would like to thank the U.S. Forest Service rangers and trail crews in Hells Canyon, the Wallowas, Umatilla National Forest, Payette National Forest, and Nez Perce National Forest, who kept us abreast of the fires and floods, helped field our questions, and reviewed our trail write-ups. We would also like to thank Mr. Ric Bailey for explaining and clarifying the role and position of the Hells Canyon Preservation Council. We are especially appreciative of the many volunteers who help keep the trails and bridges open and safe, and we would like to thank the people we passed along the trail who graciously shared their faces and thoughts with us.

Map Legend

Interstate	(95)	Hike Number	(8)
U.S. Highway	(101)	Wetland	
State or County Road	(2)	Campground	△
Forest Service Road	[7745]	Picnic Area	
Paved Road		Dam	
Gravel Road		Bridge	
Unimproved Road	=======	Building	■
Trailhead/Parking	(P)	Summit	▲ 2,477 ft
Described Trail		Mine/Quarry	✕
Alternate Trail		Viewpoint	⊙
Creek		Point of Interest	★
River		Pass/Saddle	
Body of Water		Lookout Tower	
Waterfall		Spring	

HELLS CANYON COUNTRY, OREGON

Imnaha River

Dug Bar Road

1 WENAHA RIVER TRAIL

Round trip: 19 miles (to Fairview Bar)
High point: 2,100 feet
Elevation change: 500 feet
Managed by: Pomeroy (Washington) Ranger District, Umatilla
   National Forest
Maps: USFS Wenaha-Tucannon Wilderness, USFS Umatilla National
   Forest

The scientific or ecosystem classification of Hells Canyon spans beyond
the designated boundaries of Hells Canyon National Recreation Area
and Wilderness. In the isolated Wenaha-Tucannon Wilderness Area
near the Oregon-Washington border, one also discovers the spectacular
geology and steppe-plateau habitat that helped win national recreation
area distinction for the Snake River Canyon.

Here hikers travel a remote deep-cut canyon on a parallel journey
with the Wenaha Wild and Scenic River. The tableland setting boasts
arid grassland slopes, outcrop rims, and exceptional wildlife viewing:
rocky ledges above the trail afford some of the best opportunities any-
where to observe bighorn sheep, but be alert as rattlesnakes, too, find
a niche in this rugged terrain.

Drive to the junction of OR 82 and OR 3 in Enterprise, then go north
on OR 3 toward Flora. In 32.6 miles, turn left following the well-
marked paved and gravel route to Troy. After 15.2 miles, cross the
bridge entering Troy and turn right, proceeding toward the Wenaha
Game Management Area. In 0.2 mile, turn left toward Pomeroy to
reach the marked trailhead and its pull-in parking area on the left in
another 0.3 mile.

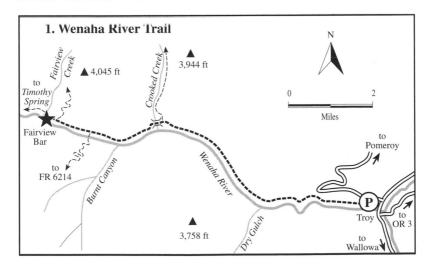

1. Wenaha River Trail

Wenaha River

For this upstream tour of the Lower Wenaha on Trail 3106, pass through the gate and briefly descend a grassy road to where a foot-path heads right. Now tour the steep grassland slope of the north canyon wall overlooking the Wenaha River. Lupine, desert parsley, balsamroot, sumac, and the occasional sprig of poison ivy decorate the sides of the trail. Hikers may also encounter areas disturbed by flood or mudslide.

Within a half mile, a ponderosa pine flat removed from the river hosts the tour; more such flats ideal for pitching a tent follow. The Wenaha River engages, flowing wide and clear even at flood stage. Riffles, small beaches, deep pools, and fish suggest river detours. Downstream views stretch to the Grande Ronde River.

Gradually, the north canyon wall transforms with rocky rims and cliffs that part the open grassland and pine-dotted slopes. At 2.6 miles, enter Umatilla National Forest. Past the 3-mile mark, a riverside bench affords the first reliable opportunity to top water jugs.

The gate at 4.5 miles (resecure upon passing) signals hikers to ready their binoculars as bighorn sheep roam the narrow ledges above the trail. The roller coaster river tour then alternates between moist, shrubby corridors and open, dry slopes. At 6 miles, enter the Wenaha-Tucannon Wilderness.

Before long the trail curves right to venture up Crooked Creek Canyon, where hikers find the Wenaha River–Panjab trail junction at 6.5 miles. For the continuation of the Wenaha River Trail, bear left crossing the Crooked Creek footbridge.

Vertical rock walls tower above the river trail while the opposite slope shows mostly forest. Ahead, this trail, too, explores a fir-pine forest with scenic cottonwoods along the shore. Views build upstream.

Amid a grassy flat at 8.6 miles, look for the Hoodoo Trail (Trail 3244) to branch left, cross the river, and mount the south canyon wall. Upstream lies Fairview Bar (9.5 miles, elevation 2,100 feet), which is the selected turnaround point.

Ponderosa pines dot the grass and bracken fern flats of Fairview Bar, which occupies a braided river stretch. Hikers may ford during low waters to obtain a south shore perspective or an alternate campsite. The Wenaha River Trail (Trail 3106/6144) continues upstream along the north shore through wilderness isolation for another 20-plus miles to Timothy Spring, appealing to the hardy and civilization-weary.

2 SPAIN SADDLE HIKE

Round trip: 6.4 miles
High point: 5,333 feet (trailhead)
Elevation change: 1,000 feet
Managed by: Hells Canyon National Recreation Area, Enterprise
Map: USFS Hells Canyon National Recreation Area

When starting from the Buckhorn Lookout Station, this hike along abandoned Eureka Road (Trail 1732) begins with a spectacular overlook of the Snake River Canyon. From the grassy summit plateau and deck-encircled observation building, take in views of the razor-edge ridges of the Imnaha River drainage. Cross-canyon looks present the Idaho side of Hells Canyon, with Seven Devils dressing the skyline.

The descent to the saddle further extols the beauty of this stunning, yet harsh realm of crisp lines, canyon folds, outcrop cliffs, plunging slopes, and terrace and temple-like features. Close-up looks at Cemetery Ridge, the Tulley and Eureka creek drainages, and Spain Saddle itself contribute to the tour.

From the OR 82–OR 3 junction in Enterprise, drive east on OR 82 for 3.3 miles and turn north on Crow Creek Road at the sign for Buckhorn Springs. After 5 miles, turn right on Zumwalt Road, a paved and improved-surface road heading toward Thomason Meadows; the road name later changes to Wellamotkin Drive/FR 46. After 31.6 miles, turn right on FR 4600.780 for Buckhorn Overlook.

Go 0.9 mile on FR 780 and bear right to reach the overlook in another 0.3 mile. This is the starting point for hikers with passenger vehicles. Hikers with high-clearance, four-wheel-drive vehicles may shorten the hike to 3.6 miles round trip by forgoing the turn to the overlook and following a far rougher FR 780 to its closure in another 1.1 miles.

Starting from the overlook, hike 0.3 mile out the entrance road and continue right on FR 780, which is, at this point, a minimally traveled dead-end two-track. Traverse the grass-and-currant vegetated plateau of Cemetery Ridge. Dispersed fir and pine dot the stage. As the slope drops away left, overlook Cherry Creek drainage, where ghost forests of fire-silvered snags fill the fingery side drainages. Glances to the right reveal the Tulley Creek and Imnaha River drainages. Free-ranging cows may share the corridor.

At 1.4 miles, reach a circular parking turnout and gate that prohibits any further vehicle use. Here hikers proceed via a livestock gate, which should be resecured after passing through. Pine needles and young grasses and plants soften the former road while rocks eroding from the slope scatter the grade.

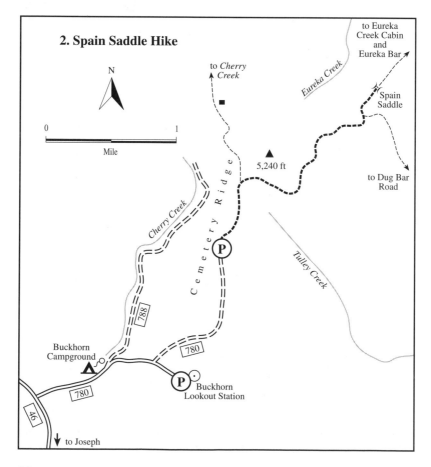

2. Spain Saddle Hike

to Eureka Creek Cabin and Eureka Bar

to Cherry Creek

N

0   1

Mile

Spain Saddle

5,240 ft

to Dug Bar Road

Eureka Creek

Cherry Creek

Cemetery Ridge

Tulley Creek

P

788

780

Buckhorn Campground

780

P Buckhorn Lookout Station

46

to Joseph

Old livestock fence

Round Tulley Creek headwaters, viewing the Imnaha River cupped in the deep fold of its canyon, shadowed by knife-edged Haas Ridge. Ocean spray, ninebark, and wild rose pepper the wildflower grassland. Willows find a niche where seeps or springs bring added moisture.

At the small saddle at 1.9 miles there is a junction. Beyond the gate to the left, locate the Cemetery Trail (Trail 1731). Bear right to continue the tour to Spain Saddle while pulling away from Cemetery Ridge.

The old road descends steadily, offering an area rarity—a carefree easy-to-follow route into the canyon wild. The only imbedded tracks betray the passage of deer. At 2.3 miles, the descent quickens. Subtle changes in direction alter perspective, as looks trend north and east.

At 2.75 miles, Tulley Creek Trail (Trail 1724) descends right, marked by a trail sign and cairn 100 feet below the road grade. It leads to Dug Bar Road, which is visible in the distance.

Soon after the trail junction, basalt knolls rise above the trail, beckoning detours for looks north and west. Keep to the old road grade to reach Spain Saddle, 3.2 miles, the suggested turnaround for most day hikers. For those who wish to continue, the trail proceeds through the saddle to contour and descend the opposite slope to Eureka Creek Cabin and Eureka Bar, a historic mining site on the Snake River.

A 150-foot scramble to the top of the saddle outcrops unites looks out Eureka Creek and across Cemetery Ridge with those of the Imnaha and Snake River drainages. Bluebirds may divert the eye, their color emphasized against the golden grassland. Views pan well into Idaho, including the famous Salmon River drainage.

3 LOWER IMNAHA RIVER TRAIL

Round trip: 10 miles (to Snake River confluence)
High point: 1,250 feet (trailhead)
Elevation change: 300 feet
Managed by: Hells Canyon National Recreation Area, Enterprise
Map: USFS Hells Canyon National Recreation Area

This trail (Trail 1713) parallels the Imnaha Wild and Scenic River through a rugged canyon setting to emerge at the Snake River confluence. While strolling the trail, revisit the canyon's mining legacy. In the 1860s, discoveries of gold lured prospectors to the area river bars. Later efforts at hard rock mining led to the rise and fall of such mining settlements as Eureka Bar, which is 1 mile north of the Imnaha-Snake River confluence and makes for a pleasant side trip.

From the town of Imnaha, drive north on County Road 735 (Lower Imnaha/Dug Bar Road) to Fence Creek where the pavement ends and the road becomes FR 4260. FR 4260 is a steep, narrow dirt road for high-clearance vehicles that passes through spectacular arid canyon scenery. Expect the road to become very slippery in wet weather. Locate the river trail at the Cow Creek bridge, 18 miles from Imnaha. Parking is on private property, so be respectful of the owner's rights and land.

Hike downstream alongside the river through a scenic, narrow canyon, with reddish-gray metamorphic rock cliffs and a sawtooth skyline. Changes in lighting animate both the Imnaha River Canyon and its squeezed side canyons. As the trail progresses, the river canyon, too, grows more pinched.

The 40- to 50-foot-wide pristine river holds a series of riffles and mesmerizing dark indigo pools. The hike follows an old, improved mining trail and generally stays some 5 feet above the river. On occasion, spring runoff or flooding may overflow onto lower portions of the trail.

In early morning and pre-evening hours, bats patrol the

Imnaha-Snake River confluence

canyon for insects. Fish ripple the water's surface. Amid the canyon rock find bunchgrass and other graminoids, alder, sumac, elderberry, prickly pear cactus, and milkweed—the food of the monarch butterfly. In places, unruly blackberry streamers or poison ivy crowd the trail. Be sure to rinse any exposed skin surfaces as soon as possible to remove the irritating ivy oils.

Mine markers, test holes, shafts, broken tools, and tailings dot both sides of the river. A signed shaft past the 4.6-mile bridge indicates the abandoned operations of Mountain Chief Mine. Cross two short spans over narrow side gorges before reaching the gravel beach of the Snake River.

Hiking north from the Imnaha-Snake River confluence leads to

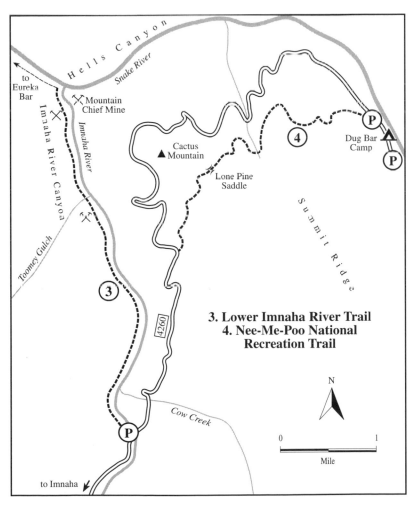

3. Lower Imnaha River Trail
4. Nee-Me-Poo National Recreation Trail

Eureka Bar, where remnant foundations hint at a one-time stamp mill and former saloon/hotel. Across the Snake River rise the stunning cliffs of Idaho.

As the canyon trail bakes in summer, an early morning start and carrying plenty of drinking water smooth the way to a more enjoyable tour. During cooler months, look for mule deer and bighorn sheep.

4 NEE-ME-POO NATIONAL RECREATION TRAIL

Round trip: 6 miles (to Lone Pine Saddle)
High point: 2,700 feet
Elevation change: 1,600 feet
Managed by: Hells Canyon National Recreation Area, Enterprise
Map: USFS Hells Canyon National Recreation Area

This hike (Trail 1721, see map p. 41) pays tribute to the Nez Perce people (Nee-Me-Poo) by retracing the portion of their historic journey that led to the Snake River crossing. In 1877, in reluctant compliance with a U.S. Army directive, Chief Joseph led his tribe through Hells Canyon en route to the Lapwai Reservation in Idaho.

Later, skirmishes with Idaho settlers persuaded the tribe to attempt a flight to Canada and freedom. A running battle ensued, spanning three months and more than 1,700 miles before the beleaguered Nez Perce surrendered.

To reach the historic trail from Imnaha, go north on County Road 735 (Lower Imnaha/Dug Bar Road) to Fence Creek where pavement ends and the road becomes FR 4260, a steep, narrow dirt road suitable only for high-clearance vehicles. Expect the road to become very slippery in wet weather; call for current road conditions. The southern trailhead, which has minimal parking, is located 21 miles from Imnaha. The northern trailhead, where parking is more readily available, is another 8 miles down the road at Dug Bar Camp. Cairns and/or signs mark both ends of the trail.

Backtracking the footsteps of the Nez Perce, from the northern trailhead, mount the slope, pass through a fence opening at 0.2 mile, and follow low rock cairns up and over the rock outcrops. Keep an eye out for these easy-to-miss cairns. At 0.4 mile a more defined footpath reveals itself. The trail then tours Hells Canyon Wilderness, traversing grassland slopes, dotted with prickly pear cactus and colored with sunflowers. Deer and chukar find suitable habitat.

The trail next dips through moist tree-lined drainages and snakes over the first of a series of saddles, delivering new perspectives on the canyon setting. Atop a second saddle at 1.2 miles, pass through a gate. A bold view of Dug Bar Road re-affirms the engineering feat of this canyon access. Here, too, hikers lose sight of the Snake River.

Lone Pine Saddle

As it descends slightly, the trail wraps around a canyon wall and past a solitary split-topped ponderosa pine before crossing a drainage and continuing its golden way. Expect steep, rugged travel in places, with game trails lending confusion.

At 3 miles the trail tops Lone Pine Saddle, which is appropriately distinguished by a single ancient lopped-top ponderosa pine. Smaller pines have since joined its ranks. As a destination, this saddle presents a spectacular vantage on the Imnaha River Canyon, Cactus Mountain, Cow and Lightning creek drainages, Corral Creek drainage, and knife-edged Haas Ridge.

From Lone Pine Saddle, the national recreation trail descends steeply on a sidewinding course to Lower Imnaha/Dug Bar Road and the southern terminus (5 miles). If you extend the tour, plan on round-trip travel as the slowness of the canyon road and limited parking do not recommend a car-shuttle.

Upon returning to the northern terminus, a short side journey upstream leads to a second piece of the historic route—Nez Perce Crossing. To access the historic river fording site, drive south from Dug Bar Camp, passing through a gate to travel a public right-of-way to the boat launch. From there, hike 0.1 mile upstream along the rocky bank of the Snake River (or just inland from the river) to the mouth of a gorge and a riverside interpretive sign.

During the forced exodus of 1877, the Nez Perce actually crossed a flooding unfettered Snake River near this site. Women, children, sick, and elderly rode atop horsehide rafts, pulled by swimming horses. Thousands of horses and cows swam the river. While the raging waters claimed great numbers of livestock, the tribe miraculously crossed without casualty.

5 SNAKE RIVER TRAIL

One-way trip: up to 48 miles (Dug Bar to Saddle Creek)
High point: 2,000 feet
Elevation change: 900 feet
Managed by: Hells Canyon National Recreation Area, Enterprise
Map: USFS Hells Canyon National Recreation Area

This grueling all-out Hells Canyon Wilderness adventure explores the west canyon wall above the Snake Wild and Scenic River. For the intrepid, this tour serves up incomparable solitude, inspiring canyon scenery, wildlife encounters, and a look at early homestead and mining efforts.

Hot and remote, Trail 1726 rolls from river bar and bench to the upper slopes and inland side canyons. Travel arid grasslands of bunchgrass, cacti, foxtail barley, sumac, and wildflowers. Expect faint, overgrown trail sections, areas of unruly poison ivy and nettles, and steep, boot-skidding descents. In deep masking grasses, be especially alert for rattlesnakes. At side-creek crossings hikers may encounter some rougher conditions because of flooding. This trail, more than any other, reveals the harsh splendor of the canyon.

Due to the trail's condition and length, chartering a boat for one leg of the journey is the best way to see more of the trail. Hikers may schedule a pick-up and drop-off between an agreed-upon ending point and Dug Bar or reverse the order for a downstream tour. Contact the recreation area or Lewiston, Idaho Chamber of Commerce for charter services.

To reach Dug Bar from Imnaha, go north on County Road 735 (Lower Imnaha/Dug Bar Road) to Fence Creek where pavement ends and the road becomes FR 4260, a steep, narrow dirt road for high-clearance vehicles only. In 30 miles, pass through a gate to reach Dug Bar boat launch and trailhead.

For an upstream hike, strike uphill from the boat launch, steer left of the corral, and cross a stair-step stile over a fence to find the trail 40 feet above the stile. Ascend steeply, drawing above Dug Bar Ranch to enter the wilderness at 1.2 miles where spectacular views of the upstream canyon are gathered. Upon crossing Fence Gulch the ascent relaxes, rounding to a saddle.

From there side-by-side horse tracks descend to the Lord Flat Trail junction (3 miles); bear left for the river trail, touring grassland to enter Dug Creek Canyon. The path, now often a mystery, crisscrosses the creek, to continue downstream through a jungle of nettles and poison ivy. A woman raised in Hells Canyon suggests a stick for just such battles.

At 4 miles, emerge near the mouth of Dug Creek for an easier, river-paired section of travel. At 4.5 miles, pass the first of several established campsites just above the river, but be aware that river travelers also vie for these.

Next comes the fording of Deep Creek (5.2 miles), a 15-foot-wide, tumbling stream and fine day hike destination. As even the named creeks may be unreliable, top water jugs at each opportunity.

The trail now contours the slope 50 feet above the river, as the canyon grows more gorge-like. A steep, difficult ascent zigzagging up Trail Gulch comes out at a saddle (6.5 miles). Thorn Creek and a nearby rustic cabin are the next landmarks encountered. At 7.8 miles, keep to the river trail rounding the slope, avoiding a trail that ascends to Deep Creek Ranch. Soon Christmas Creek Ranch contributes to the river view. Avoid the trail descending to it at 9.5 miles.

By 10 miles, begin skirting the outbuildings of abandoned Dorrance Ranch; the trail remains well above the river. Where it steeply descends the exposed north bank of Roland Creek, watch for elk. Cross the creek at 11.7 miles. Ahead, the Idaho canyon wall displays picturesque columnar basalt.

Past Cat Creek travel an overgrown grassland, detouring uphill

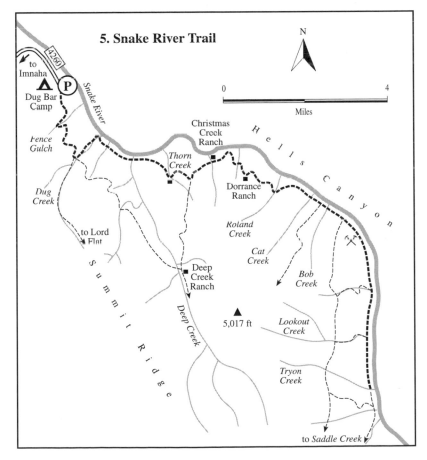

Snake River

around a private ranch. Where the trail returns to a grassy bench above the river, a tree-shaded table marks an ideal overnight stop (13 miles). Bob Creek, just upstream, is a reliable watering hole for an uncertain stretch ahead. Lone pines dot the slope.

Shortly after the Bob Creek crossing, look for cairns angling uphill around the next private holding; keep a sharp eye out as the path often disappears amid the tall grasses and sumac. Where it returns to the lower slope, look for an old mining tunnel alongside the trail.

Canyon overviews and opportunities for riverside appreciation continue, with looks at sleepy bends, riffles, rapids, and eddies. Outcrop benches, gravel bars, and isolated sandy beaches characterize the shore. Above a gravel beach at Lookout Creek reach the Tryon Creek Trail junction (17.5 miles); keep to the river trail, which crosses Tryon Creek in another 1.5 miles. A long inland stretch follows.

Hikers who make it this far have demonstrated the necessary fortitude, self-reliance, and map-reading skills to navigate the remainder of the trail on their own, should they wish to continue. Expect more of the gut-wrenching up-and-down passage through this wilderness domain and find even greater isolation.

6 CHICO TRAIL

Round trip: 10 miles (to Swamp Creek fording)
High point: 4,800 feet (trailhead)
Elevation change: 1,200 feet
Managed by: Wallowa Valley Ranger District
Map: USFS Wallowa-Whitman National Forest

Within the greater Hells Canyon Area, this hike visits the canyons of Davis and Swamp creeks, parted by Starvation Ridge, and offers opportunities for outward exploration. The hillsides present a wildflower bonanza, boasting one of the finest balsamroot displays in the state of Oregon. The end of May and early June herald the blooms. Vistas encompass the creek drainages, Starvation and Miller ridges, the picturesque high Wallowas of Oregon, and Seven Devils of Idaho. Wildlife encounters with deer, coyote, woodpecker, grouse, and vulture may enhance a tour.

As livestock range this area, be careful not to turn an ankle on a hoof-ruptured trail, and resecure gates upon passing.

From the OR 82–OR 3 junction in Enterprise, drive north on OR 3 toward Flora for 20.3 miles and turn right on FR 3000.174 for Chico Trail. From the horse staging area, proceed north on a dirt road that leads to a developed parking turnaround in 0.2 mile.

At rim's edge, pass through a hiker gate and descend the rocky, narrow footpath of Trail 1658. Hike through a meadow toward Davis Creek, which is named for the 1870s Indian interpreter, James Davis. Joseph Creek, downstream from Davis and Swamp creeks, honors the Nez Perce leader of that day—Chief Joseph.

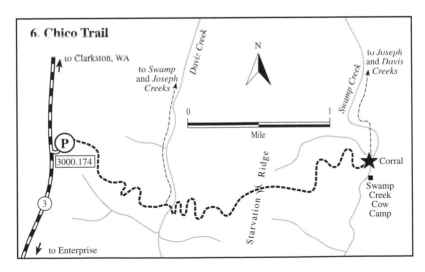

6. Chico Trail

Corral

Early views feature Starvation Ridge with the Seven Devils and high Wallowas in the distance. Springtime finds the meadow slope and forested drainages resplendent with blooms of yellow, red, blue, and purple. Desert parsley, arnica, Indian paintbrush, prairie-smoke, clover, lupine, larkspur, and phlox contribute to the display. The trail is overgrown in places and often rugged. Be sure to carry plenty of water.

After the switchbacking meadow descent, cross a small drainage and continue descending through a tight forest of small white fir, western larch, and a few mixed pine. Here violets and fairy slippers provide color.

At 1.8 miles, meet the Davis Creek Trail (Trail 1660). Downstream, the Davis Creek Trail leads to Swamp Creek, upstream FR 4602. Keep to the Chico Trail, fording Davis Creek to mount Starvation Ridge.

An open-forest and meadow tour follows, with the path sometimes faint. Nearing the ridge top at 2.7 miles, cross a jeep trail. Views feature the divided creek drainages, with Miller Ridge to the east; silvered snags hint at a fiery past.

Next skirt a cairn, pass between pines, and descend a side ridge toward Swamp Creek. In spring, a mantle of vibrant green dresses the hillside; by fall, the robe turns golden. At 3.3 miles, cross over this side ridge, trading up-canyon views for downstream ones.

The descent quickens near the forested foot of the slope. Beyond the gate at 4.6 miles, vegetation again overwhelms the trail. Head downstream along a fence line and keep a sharp eye toward Swamp Creek, looking for the next trail sign tacked to a ponderosa pine (4.7 miles). From the sign, follow the Swamp Creek Trail (Trail 1678) downstream toward Joseph Creek, passing through a corral to the chosen turn-around site—the fording at 5 miles. Cross-creek views present Miller Ridge.

To extend the tour, hikers may follow the Swamp Creek Trail upstream less than a mile to Swamp Creek Cow Camp before turning around. Or, by fording Swamp Creek and hiking downstream, they may loop back via the Davis Creek Trail for a 19.4-mile round-trip tour. At the north end of Starvation Ridge (10.3 miles), make a dual fording of Swamp and Davis creeks, and look for a rusting sign on a ponderosa pine. Although no longer readable, this sign marks the upstream return. The trail contours the western slope well above Davis Creek, returning to the cairn marking the Chico Trail junction. From the cairn strike uphill to the trailhead.

7 GRANNY VIEW AND HAT POINT INTERPRETIVE TRAILS

Loop trip: 0.5 mile for each of the two trails
High point: 6,345 feet (Granny View); 6,982 feet (Hat Point)
Elevation change: minimal (Granny View); 150 feet (Hat Point)
Managed by: Hells Canyon National Recreation Area, Enterprise
Map: USFS Hells Canyon National Recreation Area

These recently constructed loop trails offer what are perhaps the finest Hells Canyon views on the western rim, as well as welcome leg-stretches when touring Hat Point Road Scenic Drive.

From Imnaha, go southeast on FR 4240/Hat Point Road, a winding gravel single-lane road with turnouts. At 16 miles, turn right for trail parking for Granny View Interpretive Trail. Trailhead parking for Hat Point Lookout and Interpretive Trail is available at the end of FR 4240 (22.3 miles).

Find the loop junction near the trailhead sign for the cinder-surfaced **Granny View Interpretive Trail**; proceed forward for a counter-clockwise tour. The loop explores the arid niche-habitats of the rim while securing tree-framed and open overlooks of the stirring Imnaha River Canyon. Admire the river canyon's fluted and basalt-tiered slopes and green riparian ribbon, along with the purple horizon of the distant Blue Mountains. Elsewhere, view the converging canyons of Freezeout Creek and Imnaha River, as the majestic Wallowas shoot up in the distance.

Interpretive panels explain the microclimates of the rim. Larkspur, paintbrush, and buckwheat sprinkle springtime color while ninebark,

Hells Canyon from Hat Point

young aspen, snowberry, and Rocky Mountain maple bring accents of fall. A few spired subalpine firs and wind-shaped Douglas-firs dot the grassland-shrub habitat, their branches frequented by squirrels, songbirds, and gray jays. Eagle and vulture sail the thermals, and lichen and moss grow amid the small basalt outcrops.

Boardwalks span the steeper dropping slopes, with benches welcoming a lengthier study of this landscape of striking contrast and vertical relief. Views span a 25-mile distance.

Hat Point Interpretive Trail starts below the lookout and to the right of its trailhead kiosk. A ghostly forest left behind from a 1989 lightning-caused fire spreads outward. Fireweed and other renewing species regenerate the slope.

In 100 feet, the path to the left offers a direct route to the lookout; keep right both here and at the upcoming junction at 0.1 mile to tour

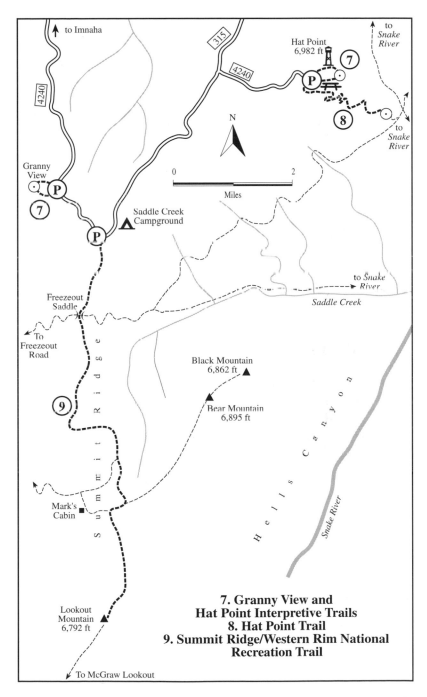

to Imnaha

315

4240

Hat Point
6,982 ft

7

P

to
Snake
River

8

to
Snake
River

N

Granny
View

P

7

Saddle Creek
Campground

0   2

Miles

Freezeout
Saddle

To
Freezeout
Road

to Snake
River

Saddle Creek

Summit Ridge

Hells Canyon

9

Black Mountain
6,862 ft

Bear Mountain
6,895 ft

Snake River

Mark's
Cabin

Lookout
Mountain
6,792 ft

To McGraw Lookout

**7. Granny View and
Hat Point Interpretive Trails
8. Hat Point Trail
9. Summit Ridge/Western Rim National
Recreation Trail**

the full loop. The interpretive loop travels the outskirts of the fir-shaded picnic area, stopping at vistas that build anticipation for a lookout visit. Panels explain the area geology.

A round-up of views begins with an overlook of the Saddle Creek drainage, the disturbing beauty of Hells Canyon proper, and Idaho's impressive Seven Devils. Looks trend north, adding cross-canyon scenes of Idaho's Heavens Gate Lookout and Ridge.

The circuit passes above Hat Point Trail (Trail 1752) and offers a platform overlook of Rush Creek Rapids before following a thin cindery footpath uphill to the right, reaching the lookout. Hat Point Lookout, a 90-foot-high fire tower, stands more than a vertical mile above the twisting Snake River (elevation 1,250 feet). Take in the scenery from a lower-tower viewing deck or from the midway platform. When staffed and when the stairway gate is open, the public may venture to the crow's nest.

The 360-degree view sweeps the golden slopes, knife-edge ridges, and deep finger drainages of Hells Canyon; the Wallowa Valley tapestry; and the Blues, Wallowas, and Seven Devils. On deck, an Osborne firefinder and explanatory panel help visitors focus on locations of interest. When you are ready to depart, a counterclockwise rounding of the tower delivers a direct descent to the trailhead parking area (0.5 mile).

8   HAT POINT TRAIL

Round trip: 5 miles (to vista point)
High point: 6,900 feet (trailhead)
Elevation change: 1,600 feet
Managed by: Hells Canyon National Recreation Area, Enterprise
Map: USFS Hells Canyon National Recreation Area

Hat Point indirectly derives its name from a nearby creek, where an errant cowboy hat that lay wedged in a bush suggested the name "Hat Creek" to early canyon residents. This trail (Trail 1752, see map p. 51) reveals the steepness of the canyon flanks and offers a perspective from within Hells Canyon, which differs from that gained along the neighboring rim trails. While traversing the dry meadows, enjoy peak wildflower bloom in early summer.

Much of the trail is shadeless, so timing a hike for early morning or evening hours promises a more comfortable outing. Carry plenty of drinking water—none is available along Hat Point Road or the trail—and watch footing.

From Imnaha, drive southeast on FR 4240/Hat Point Road, a winding gravel single-lane road with turnouts, and follow it to its end at 22.3 miles. This necessarily slow road allows travelers to enjoy the scenery, vistas, and area wildlife. Begin the hike at the marked loading dock and trailhead on the right, prior to reaching the lookout area parking lot.

Gnarled snag

The trail contours the slope north for 0.1 mile, coming to a trail register below Hat Point Interpretive Trail and Picnic Area. A winding descent from the West Rim follows, passing through dry, high-elevation meadows. Buckwheat and larkspur lend early-season color. By autumn, asters and Indian paintbrush adorn the golden-russet grassland, gone to seed.

Sweeping vistas of the canyon, with its furrowed flanks and basalt terraces, preface the Hells Canyon Wilderness at 0.5 mile. Upon entering the wilderness area, switchbacks pass between forest and dry meadow habitats. Ponderosa pine, some Douglas-fir, a few small Rocky Mountain maples, and mountain mahogany contribute to the tree cover. The switchback at 1.9 miles and its accompanying northern view suggest an alternate turnaround.

At 2.25 miles views extend south and east. By 2.4 miles, the forest grows fuller and wetter, supporting twisted stalk, thimbleberry, nettles, and bracken fern.

Just ahead, detour 50 feet off-trail onto an open, sun-basked gravelly plateau, with one side dropping steeply away. Here find an exceptional vista of the downstream river course and the enfolding canyon grasslands, bluffs, and orange spired cliffs. Also overlook the next lower plateau, rising where Waterspout Creek and Smooth Hollow meet. A few mountain mahogany cling to the vantage cliff; yellow and green lichen color the rock.

For day hikers, this 2.5-mile site signals an ideal turnaround point after having discovered the views, experienced the steepness of the terrain, and witnessed various canyon habitats. For the hardier, the descent continues, meeting High Trail (Trail 1751) in another mile and the Snake River (elevation 1,250 feet) in another 4 miles.

9 SUMMIT RIDGE/WESTERN RIM NATIONAL RECREATION TRAIL

Round trip: 18 miles to Lookout Mountain
High point: 6,800 feet
Elevation change: 1,400 feet
Managed by: Hells Canyon National Recreation Area, Enterprise
Map: USFS Hells Canyon National Recreation Area

This hike (Trail 1774, see map p. 51) traces the Hells Canyon Wilderness boundary along the western rim, unveiling the harsh beauty of the arid-steppe wilds and winning vistas of the deep-cut canyons of the Imnaha and Snake rivers. Views range from Oregon's high Wallowas in the distant southwest to Idaho's Seven Devils in the east.

Peak blooms arrive in early summer. In autumn, a scenic array of gold and russet seed pods lends interest to an outing. Isolated and untamed, Hells Canyon calls to the adventurous, not the foolhardy. Exercise full caution, be alert for rattlesnakes, and carry plenty of water. In places, the trail grows faint.

From Imnaha, drive 17 miles southeast on FR 4240/Hat Point Road, a slow single-lane gravel road, to find Jim Spring Trailhead on the right. Park to the side of the road or uphill at Saddle Creek Campground.

This rugged and often rocky national recreation trail (NRT) wraps around and down a ridge, offering early views of the Imnaha River and Freezeout Creek drainages. Buckwheat, bunchgrass, balsamroot, and fireweed contribute to the open, dry slope, as do a few fir and silvered snags. At 0.8 mile, watch for where the trail angles back to descend the eastern slope overlooking the Snake River Canyon.

At 1.5 miles, cross back onto the western side of the ridge, traveling a beautiful meadow of native bunchgrass to Freezeout Saddle and its 4-way junction (2.2 miles). Here the NRT traces the ridge straight ahead to McGraw Lookout; a second trail heads left along Saddle Creek, reaching the Snake River; and a third trail heads right toward Freezeout Road. Southeastern views pair smooth-sided Bear Mountain with the rocky cliffs of Black Mountain.

Continue straight to traverse a bunchgrass-wildflower slope just below the ridge top that overlooks Freezeout Canyon. The trail loses its cant and much of the rock. Where the ridge dips to meet the trail at 2.7 miles, steal a quick look at Hat Point Lookout.

A contouring ascent follows. Alternately tour picturesque grassland and transitioning tree-shrub habitat. Rounding a bend at 3.5 miles, exchange looks at Freezeout Saddle for ones of Imnaha Canyon and the distant Wallowas. With the next direction change, enjoy an over-the-shoulder look tracing Freezeout Creek to its Imnaha River confluence; each bend holds variety.

At 5.3 miles pass below a recovering burn habitat, with standing snags and young evergreens. Beyond a fence passage, meet Trail 1763 and proceed forward for the NRT to admire Idaho's Seven Devils beyond Bear Mountain.

Downed snags and sprouting aspen record a burn on the western slope. At 6.6 miles, Bear Mountain Trail (Trail 1743) heads left while the NRT bears right. Below this junction, a seasonal spring feeds an area of green; watch for wildlife.

Before long, an old jeep trail hosts the tour. Where it meets a second jeep trail at 6.9 miles, bear left for Lookout Mountain. Downhill to the right 0.5 mile is Mark's Cabin, now sealed. On the NRT, return to undisturbed grassland edged by forest and punctuated by lily, sagebrush, and lupine.

Keep to the rim trail for a long, gentle ascent to the summit of Lookout Mountain (9 miles), with its radio tower and mostly treed flank. Although trees deny a 360-degree view, the top does extend a fine Hells Canyon panorama for a satisfying ending. Rim travelers may continue 9 miles more to McGraw Lookout.

Packers at Freezeout Saddle

Snake River below Stud Creek

10   STUD CREEK TRAIL

Round trip: 2 miles
High point: 1,600 feet
Elevation change: 100 feet
Managed by: Hells Canyon National Recreation Area, Enterprise
Map: USFS Hells Canyon National Recreation Area

From the Hells Canyon Creek boat launch, Stud Creek Trail (Trail 1781) journeys north downstream along the western shore of the Snake River. It presents a glimpse at the region's Native American past, as well as stunning river, canyon, and side-canyon viewing. Bring scopes or binoculars for cross-canyon looks that may hold sightings of mountain goats or bighorn sheep, particularly in winter and spring. The animals seek higher range in summer.

While built to withstand high water, the trail may show evidence of the flood of 1997. Throughout the tour, be alert for showings of poison ivy and even rattlesnakes.

To reach Stud Creek Trail, from Halfway, Oregon, follow OR 86 east. At the Oxbow junction in 16 miles, proceed straight, cross the Snake River bridge into Idaho, and bear left on the east shore road, following signs for Hells Canyon Dam. From Idaho, reach the east shore road 40 miles northwest of Cambridge via ID 71.

Continue another 22 miles, cross the dam, and drive north on the Oregon shore for 1 mile to reach Hells Canyon Creek Boat Launch and

Visitor Center and the trailhead. As the visitor center lacks drinking water, top off water containers at Hells Canyon Park, an Idaho Power facility on the east shore that is located on the left en route to the dam.

The trail's start is off of the back porch of the visitor center. Descend the stairway and bear left away from the boat launch to begin the hike. Cross Hells Canyon Creek, a picturesque series of stepped cascades spilling to the Snake River. Trees and shrubs crowd its banks, as do water-fanned tangles of poison ivy.

Next, travel a boardwalk to study a depression left by a Hells Canyon Creek pit house, a dwelling shaped of poles and reeds. To the site's north, a set of stairs ascends to the charred overhang of a rock shelter used by early Native American hunters.

The Wild and Scenic Snake River accompanies this tour, flowing freely below the dam. As the canyon walls fold together, admire picturesque river bends and the bulging, broken, unruly rock that dominates the terrain. The Snake flows big, wide, and brownish, with white riffles, smooth eddies, and Cliff Mountain Rapids midway

Wildflowers—campion, bluebells, mullein, and larkspur—adorn the arid western slope. Sumac, currant, gooseberry, and the often dead-looking hackberry number among the shrubs. Despite its civilized features, this sun-drenched, mildly rolling trail provides a good introduction to the rigors and beauty of Hells Canyon travel.

At 0.3 mile, round a rocky cove with an access spur to the river. Here looms a cliff with dark recesses, overhangs, and fissures. Farther north, a handful of pines dot a scenic point.

Where planed outcrops separate the trail from the river, enjoy prized seating 25 feet above the water. Skyline trees provide a sense of scale to the imposing rim heights that frame up and downstream views.

Showy yellow monkey flowers adorn the seeps in a rock face at 0.6 mile. An uphill switchback then doubles the vertical height between river and trail. The trail rolls between river and rise to traverse a grassy inland plateau, decked in balsamroot.

At 0.9 mile, cross a side-fork stream via stepping stones, and soon after come to the rocky shore at the mouth of Stud Creek, where the hike ends.

HELLS CANYON CREEK TRAIL

Round trip: 0.5 mile
High point: 1,600 feet
Elevation change: 100 feet
Managed by: Hells Canyon National Recreation Area, Enterprise
Map: USFS Hells Canyon National Recreation Area

This hike ventures through the narrow chasm of the original Hells Canyon, so named by early miners. Measuring but 100 feet wide and enfolded by canyon walls shooting 2,000 feet skyward, this cataract

Hells Canyon Creek

only briefly captures the light of day. Threaded by the sparkling ribbon of Hells Canyon Creek, the gash shows a bounty of green and captivates onlookers with an elegant two-stage waterfall. With multiple creek crossings, this hike is best tackled during low water.

From Halfway, Oregon, drive east on OR 86 for 16 miles and continue straight at the Oxbow junction, cross the bridge into Idaho, and bear left to follow signs for Hells Canyon Dam. From Idaho, reach Oxbow junction 40 miles northwest of Cambridge, taking ID 71. Go north 22 miles, cross the dam, and continue north another mile on the Oregon shore to reach Hells Canyon Creek Boat Launch and Visitor Center. The trail is at the base of a set of stairs at the upper end of the visitor center parking lot. Bring drinking water as none is available at the center.

Enter the deep, pinched side canyon of Hells Canyon Creek for an upstream tour to the falls. Dark, steep volcanic cliffs enclose the tour. Amid the ledges, hollows, and gaps grow grasses, moss, and shrubs. Alder, maple, gooseberry, currant, miner's lettuce, and moss color the riparian zone green.

Continue upstream alongside the creek, passing two eye-socket hollows at the base of the cliff. Smoke blackens the overhangs, perhaps hinting at their past use as shelters. Just beyond the hollows, look for the first creek crossing. Depending on season, hikers may need to wade, rock-hop, or pace off a log. Although short, the trail has always had an undeniable cross-country flavor. With the flood of 1997, it officially crossed over.

Where the canyon grows pinched, showing a jutting north wall, the south shore offers the low-water option for reaching the falls, crisscrossing the creek several times. In times of high water, reduce the number of crossings by keeping to the north shore: after a steep, difficult rock scramble, share a preview look at Hells Canyon Creek Falls before hopscotching back and forth across the creek to the base of the lower falls. Fragments of foot trail may aid hikers.

The lower falls plummets some 25 feet, with its broad, shimmery veil parting around protruding cliff. Dippers favor the remoteness of the falls; in spring, watch for an active pair to dart in and out of the shower, visiting a nest secure beneath the overhang.

As the site's massive boulder and sheer canyon walls successfully shape a box canyon, best looks at the upper falls are those gathered while clambering over the slope and rock of the north wall. Be careful when making the scramble and crossing the creek on wet stones.

12 BUCK CREEK–32 POINT– BENCH TRAILS LOOP

Loop trip: 6.3 miles
High point: 6,141 feet
Elevation change: 2,150 feet
Managed by: Hells Canyon National Recreation Area, Enterprise
Map: USFS Hells Canyon National Recreation Area

Joining parts of three trails below Buck Point Overlook, this wilderness loop along the western flank of Hells Canyon presents the rigors, challenge, and beauty of this untameable landscape. Narrow footpaths travel grassland slopes and rims and visit a surprisingly rich drainage of fir and old-growth ponderosa pine.

Beware of loose gravel and treacherously steep grades: in places, hikers may need to scan the slope ahead to discern the line of travel, and elsewhere false paths introduce confusion. Be sure to carry plenty of water.

From Wallowa Mountain Loop Road/FR 39 (43 miles southeast of Joseph; 29 miles northeast of Halfway), drive east on FR 3965 for Hells Canyon Overlook. In 2.6 miles, find the paved road to the overlook. After that point, FR 3965 is suitable only for high-clearance vehicles. A cairn marks the Bench Trail, found along a jeep trail that heads right off FR 3965, 7 miles past Hells Canyon Overlook. Travel another half mile on FR 3965 to find the Buck Creek Trailhead. Start at the latter for the easier-to-follow clockwise tour.

Round left behind the cairn for Buck Creek Trail (Trail 1788) for a sharp descent on a gravel-soiled grassland slope adorned by balsamroot, paintbrush, pungent herbs, and bunchgrass. At 0.2 mile take the first switchback on a fir-shaded point. Views now vacillate between Buck Creek Canyon to the south and 32 Point drainage and Seven Devils to the north.

Nearing the upper drainage of Buck Creek find maples, cherries,

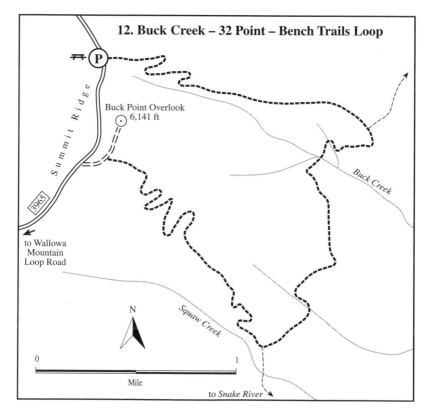

12. Buck Creek – 32 Point – Bench Trails Loop

Summit Ridge

Buck Point Overlook
6,141 ft

3965

Buck Creek

to Wallowa
Mountain
Loop Road

N

Squaw Creek

0   1
Mile

to Snake River

Ponderosa pine

and other shrubs. Uphill to the left, bumpy basalt accents the slope. By 0.9 mile, win a reprieve from the steep descent as the trail contours the north canyon wall of Buck Creek, gradually drawing atop the declining ridge (1.2 miles) for a more measured descent.

The trail then twists downhill amid outcrops, keeping to the north side of the rim. Overlook 32 Point drainage, with its basalt-tiered steppes and steep treed creases. Where the trail wanes at a small grassy flat at 2 miles, stay alert. Find the 32 Point Trail junction in the pine grove as you exit the flat. For the loop, locate the trail swinging right (south); avoid taking the path to the left, which is marked by an inconspicuous trail sign 20 feet into the grove.

Southbound, the 32 Point Trail (Trail 1789) descends into the for-ested drainage of Buck Creek, to tour a flat of giant ponderosa pines at 2.4 miles. At an unmarked junction along a side creek, turn right and hike upstream to the crossing (2.6 miles). Cross main Buck Creek in another 0.1 mile; both streams are dry in summer.

A steep ascent amid mixed firs and pine leads to the next grassy ridge at 3 miles. A ponderosa pine to the right of the trail holds a sign that reads "32 Point Trail." Take a couple of strides forward and look for the trail to arc left, contouring and descending south along the western slope. Grasshoppers enliven the grassland; Summit Ridge rises to the right.

Balsamroot

At the nose of the ridge, descend to a treed drainage north of Squaw Creek, parallel its channel downstream, and cross at 3.6 miles. Next enter a handsome grassy flat dispersed with pines. Here grouse, magpie, and Steller's jays serve up entertainment.

Here, too, come upon the next unmarked fork (3.75 miles). Bear left along the lower slope, quickly coming upon a signed trail junction with the Bench Trail (Trail 1884). For the loop, turn right (west), following the Bench Trail uphill to Summit Ridge.

Trace a straight line west from the junction pine to find the Bench Trail taking shape farther up slope. Travel a shrub-pine habitat along the southern slope, overlooking the snag-pierced young forest of Squaw Creek. Woody vegetation congests the trail but the path remains fairly obvious.

Where the trail follows low cairns across a grassy pine slope, stay alert for a switchback to the right. Avoid the tracked path ahead that resumes amid shrubs. A steep, weaving ascent follows, with a few pines for prized shade. Craggy basalt, sage-grasslands, and twisted mountain mahogany add to the trail's character.

Where vegetation becomes sparse, the trail may disappear; watch for cairns. With the climb, regain looks toward Seven Devils, with cross-canyon views of the Kinney Creek drainage and Horse Mountain Lookout.

By 5 miles the traveled ridge melds into the steep upper slope, branded by calf-straining switchbacks. At 5.7 miles enter a strip of firs before reaching the Bench Trail cairn off FR 3965 (5.8 miles). Look west for the Wallowas.

Here descend the jeep trail and turn right on FR 3965 to close the loop at Buck Creek Trailhead (6.3 miles). Or, hike the jeep trail uphill 0.1 mile to Buck Point Overlook and a panel on the ill-fated Bonneville Expedition of 1834. During that winter, conditions forced the four-man party to abandon its Hells Canyon exploration and mount a grueling climb over the Snake-Imnaha Divide.

From the sign, descend to FR 3965 and bear right to close the loop.

Hells Canyon Reservoir

13   HELLS CANYON RESERVOIR TRAIL

Round trip: 3 miles (to McGraw Creek)
High point: 1,800 feet
Elevation change: 200 feet
Managed by: Hells Canyon National Recreation Area, Enterprise
Map: USFS Hells Canyon National Recreation Area

Enfolded by the humbling vertical walls of Hells Canyon, Trail 1890 along the west river bench offers engaging Snake River overlooks and visits a series of sparkling side streams. A downstream dam fetters this portion of the Snake River to shape Hells Canyon Reservoir. Boat traffic, passing waterfowl, and evening bats share the canyon corridor.

From I-84 north of Baker City, take OR 86 east for 52 miles to Half-way, where gas and services are available. Then continue east on OR 86 toward the Snake River. At Copperfield Park in 16 miles, follow the narrow single-lane gravel road heading north (downstream) along the Oregon side of the river for 8.7 miles to road's end and the trailhead.

The narrow road is suitable for passenger vehicles, but take it slow. In the absence of a developed parking area, park to the side of the road. Avoid private property near and along the trail.

Step over the low fence at road's end and cross intermittent Copper Creek to begin this northbound tour. The rolling trail vacillates between 5 and 70 feet above the Snake River. A variety of herbs, forbs, and shrubs vegetate the arid western slope. Discover sumac, sage, wild rose, bitterbrush, and thistle, with poison ivy in the moister nooks. Yellow, red, white, and blue wildflowers spangle the hillside. In early morning and pre-evening hours, watch for deer making their way to or from the water.

Cross-canyon views pay tribute to the Idaho shore—a vertical landscape of dry hillsides, scenic crags, basalt summit rims, and greenery-filled drainages. In July, shimmery fins pierce the water as spawning carp collect in pools just below the reservoir's surface.

Nelson Creek next marks off distance. It is slightly larger than Copper Creek and has a bit of shade. The trail then climbs and proceeds through a gate; resecure it upon passing. Lichen-etched rock outcrops and cliffs intersperse the grassland.

At McGraw Creek (1.5 miles), encounter a more prominent black-cliff canyon. Admire the sawtooth skyline, grassland slopes, and a picturesque delta and welcoming beach where the creek spills into a quiet arm of Hells Canyon Reservoir.

Upon crossing McGraw Creek, keep to the river trail, staying low along shore. Floods have now stolen most of a trail that ventured up McGraw Creek Canyon to McGraw Cabin. At the side-creek crossings on the Hells Canyon Reservoir Trail, hikers also may have noticed the impacts of flooding.

Gradually the trail rolls higher up the slope, as it approaches the boundary for Hells Canyon National Recreation Area; Spring Creek Canyon lies beyond. This large canyon will have been in sight since the start of the hike, but a thick rush of vegetation, including an explosion of poison ivy, may deny access. Often continuation of the tour requires recent trail maintenance or a bold spirit.

Hikers who push forward into the recreation area soon come upon the marked Bench Trail (Trail 1884), which charges left uphill to Summit Ridge in 10 miles. Bear right to continue the river tour, fording Spring Creek at 2 miles. A rock slide bars hiking past Leep Creek (5 miles).

HELLS CANYON COUNTRY, IDAHO

Seven Devils Trail

14   MEXICAN HAT TRAIL

Round trip: 0.2 mile
High point: 1,300 feet
Elevation change: none
Managed by: Hells Canyon National Recreation Area, Riggins
Map: USFS Hells Canyon National Recreation Area

This short interpretive trail visits a prized archaeological resource featuring a unique sombrero-shaped rock highly decorated with Native American petroglyphs (etched drawings). To protect this site, state police and U.S. Forest Service personnel make spot checks. All trail users, however, must share in the responsibility of protecting this rare, irreplaceable treasure. Keep to the trail, admire but refrain from touching the art, and take only photographs as mementos. Travel respectfully as the site holds special significance to the canyon's Native American people.

From US 95 1.2 miles south of the White Bird Junction (17 miles south of Grangeville), turn west at a sign for Hammer Creek and Pittsburg Landing. Cross the Salmon River in 0.9 mile, and immediately turn left on Deer Creek Road/County 493 for Pittsburg Landing. Stay on County 493, a graveled road, and proceed straight at intersections. In 10.5 miles reach Pittsburg Saddle and Hells Canyon National Recreation Area.

Ahead find a single-lane road with a 16-percent grade and blind

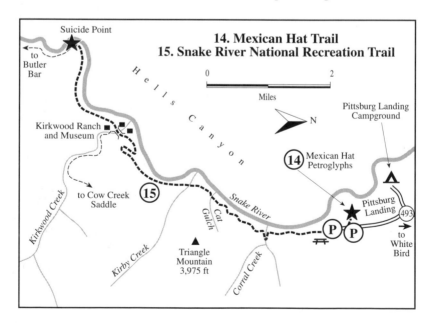

14. Mexican Hat Trail
15. Snake River National Recreation Trail

curves; use a low gear and yield to uphill traffic. From Pittsburg Saddle, drive 5.6 miles and turn left on a paved single-lane road to Upper Landing and the petroglyphs. Parking for Mexican Hat is on the right in 0.9 mile. An interpretive panel marks the trail's start.

On a plateau above the Snake River, the graveled, wheelchair-accessible interpretive trail travels a picturesque boulder-strewn hackberry-grassland to visit the aptly named "Mexican Hat." This unmistakable rock bears an intriguing array of petroglyph images, dating back thousands of years. Petroglyphs represent the oldest form of Native American art found in the recreation area. Elsewhere, pictographs (rock paintings) and scratchings may be spied.

In 100 feet at the loop junction, the trail parts around Mexican Hat and two other picture rocks. Rainwater catches in the trough of the rock's sombrero brim; the top of Mexican Hat bears a mortar depression. Designs consist of stick figures, squiggles, dotted lines, and circles.

On nearby rocks, centuries of weathering, the growth of lichen, and the dark natural varnish of time have rendered some of the images barely detectable. Perhaps half a dozen petroglyph rocks grace the circuit; keep an eye out for them.

Rabbits, meadowlarks, crickets, and ladybugs enliven a tour. In season, wildflowers decorate the grassland. The inspiring canyon backdrop and companion Snake River song contribute to the extraordinary site. Even on this short walk, be alert for ticks and snakes.

Mexican Hat petroglyphs

67

Snake River near Kirby Bar

15 SNAKE RIVER NATIONAL RECREATION TRAIL

Round trip: 17 miles (to Suicide Point)
High point: 1,600 feet
Elevation change: 300 feet
Managed by: Hells Canyon National Recreation Area, Riggins
Map: USFS Hells Canyon National Recreation Area

Parallel long-distance trails travel the Idaho and Oregon shores of the Snake River. The more civilized tour on the Idaho shore (Trail 102, see map p. 66) holds national recreation trail distinction while the more challenging trail of the Oregon shore does not.

Rolling along the east bank and wall of Hells Canyon, the Idaho tour extends captivating river overlooks, provides an intimate canyon perspective, and visits historic Kirkwood Ranch on the National Register of Historic Places. Suicide Point adds an element of drama to the hike: legend has it that from this promontory a Native American "Romeo and Juliet," one Shoshone, the other Nez Perce, tied their braids together and jumped to their deaths.

From US 95 1.2 miles south of White Bird Junction (17 miles south of Grangeville), turn west for Pittsburg Landing, cross the Salmon River, and turn left on Deer Creek Road/County 493. Stay on graveled

68

County 493 to reach Pittsburg Saddle and Hells Canyon National Recreation Area in 10.5 miles. Ahead lies a twisting, steep single-lane road; use a low gear and yield to uphill traffic. From the saddle, go 5.6 miles and turn left on the paved single-lane road to Upper Landing. Reach the trailhead in 1.6 miles. Water is not available.

Hike south (upstream) from the end of the parking lot reaching an information board and register. A narrow, well-defined foot trail then contours the canyon slope some 100 feet above the river, passing through a hackberry-grassland. Shortly after, the trail ascends while rounding the foot of a rugged volcanic slope. Expect steep pitches and boot-skidding rock even on this superior leg of the national recreation trail (NRT). Poison ivy has a spotty presence but thrives in side-canyon gulches.

At 0.4 mile, top a point for admiring looks at the yawning canyon below Pittsburg Landing and at the pinched canyon upstream. Traverse a river bar to the Corral Creek crossing (1 mile), which is generally an early-season wading. China Creek Rapids agitate the Snake River, and an off-trail boulder scramble allows river access.

Prickly pear cactus, balsamroot, sumac, horehound, paintbrush, and a succession of wildflowers decorate the tour. The inner canyon engages with its cliffs, rocks, and grassland bars. Where the walls fold together admire the backset rims. Views are constant and subtly change with each river bend.

At 1.7 miles, the route drifts inland alongside an old fence. At a fork with an unmaintained trail, the Snake River Trail proceeds up the hill to round some 200 feet above the river. Phlox adorns the rock of the slope; wild hyacinth the grassland. Meadowlark, magpie, deer, and chukar commonly raise diversion while massive tangled nests draw attention to the hackberry bushes. At 2.4 miles, round through a small gulch above Lower Kirby Rapids.

A half mile past Cat Gulch, look for the trail to curve inland, following a rustic fence around a private inholding. At 3.5 miles, cross Kirby Creek to pass through a picturesque u-shaped saddle. Scree chutes interrupt the grassland, and bold overlooks of the river return.

Rounding a point at 5.1 miles, overlook the long pasture and primitive campsites of Kirkwood Ranch. Steep switchbacks descend to the historic ranch; be attentive to footing. Enter the gate (5.6 miles) and follow a mowed swath south through the pasture to reach the buildings, museum, and a self-guiding walking tour. Fliers from the museum and interpretive signs explain the history and lay of the ranch.

The ranch is a pleasant stop-over for the night or part of the day. At the site there are compost toilets but no potable water. Avoid taking drinking water from the river, and treat all water from side-creek sources. An annual campfire ban is in effect July 1 through mid-September and during times of fire danger. When fires are allowed, use a firepan and pack out ash.

Upon crossing the Kirkwood Creek footbridge, a sign points the way for thru-trail hikers. A small waterwheel and flume operate nearby. Black hawthorn, mock orange (syringa), chokecherry, red birch, and elderberry crowd the stream banks.

Resume the river tour amid the ranch equipment display. Where the

NRT passes through a fence section (6 miles), a 100-foot side spur heads left to a simple grave marker semi-buried in the grass. Emerging from a gate, the NRT follows a footpath left; avoid the jeep track descending to the river.

The rolling tour resumes 50 feet above the river. Travel from rocky terrain to grassland, gradually drawing farther from the river. The terrain denies river access, as a few old mileage markers count off distance. Upstream, view the plummeting outcrop of Suicide Point; cross-river views find historic Salt Creek Cabin.

The apex of Suicide Point is reached at 8.5 miles. Here view the picturesque plateau of Big Bar upstream, the traveled canyon downstream, and the perilous cliffs below. While this site marks the chosen turnaround, hikers may continue upstream all the way to Butler Bar, another 22 miles distant.

16   BOISE TRAIL, NORTH

Round trip: 7.2 miles (to the Narrows)
High point: 8,000 feet
Elevation change: 1,000 feet
Managed by: Hells Canyon National Recreation Area, Riggins
Map: USFS Hells Canyon National Recreation Area

This hike follows part of the historic Boise Trail (Trail 101), a primary north-south route through rugged western Idaho used first by Native Americans and later by explorers and prospectors. Today, the boots of contemporary travelers plod the well-tried canyon route. Delight in vistas spanning four states, encounter pika and hawk, enjoy wildflower diversity, and come to appreciate the steep grassland slopes of Hells Canyon.

Expect an open, shadeless tour. Carry water (none is available at the trailhead), wear sun-protection, and watch for building thunderstorms; the open ridge is a dangerous place to get caught.

To reach the northbound Boise Trail from Riggins, drive south on US 95 for 1.3 miles and turn right on improved-surface Squaw Creek Road for Seven Devils Campground; camp trailers and recreational vehicles are not permitted. In 1.6 miles bear left, and in another 7.4 miles, turn right on Seven Devils Road/FR 517, following the signs. FR 517 typically opens for travel in early to mid-July.

The road ahead becomes rough, but remains passable for passenger vehicles with good clearance and reliable tires; go slow. In 7 miles at Windy Saddle, bear right at the junction for Heavens Gate Vista. The northbound Boise Trail leaves the vista area parking in 1.6 miles.

Hike north from the vista parking area; a sign marks the Boise Trail. The trail contours the canyon slope overlooking Hells Canyon to reach a small ridge feature and knob at 0.2 mile. Find east-west views out the Salmon and Snake River drainages. Distant peaks stretch east to the Montana border.

Grassland slope on Boise Trail

The trail passes through scenic high-elevation meadows and twisted-tree habitat. Whitebark pines, skirted firs, and white snags shape wooded pockets. The open meadows abound with bunchgrass, lupine, buckwheat, aster, phlox, and yarrow. More protected areas show dwarf huckleberry and Jacob's ladder.

The Boise Trail traverses Heavens Gate Ridge rolling from ridge top to saddle and from west flank to east flank. Heavens Gate Lookout on its cliff top perch cuts a striking profile to the south. The open, steep-meadow slopes afford unobstructed views. Where rocky knoll and jumbles top the rise, watch for pikas—those cute, big-eared balls of fur with high-pitched squeaks of warning.

By 1.4 miles, the trail rounds above Papoose Lake, a green mountain pool below the trail that is isolated by a 200-foot cliff. Grouse and deer may cross paths with hikers. In 1996, the Heavens Gate fire swept this part of the trail, charring trees in a hit-and-miss pattern and revitalizing the grassland. Within a week of the fire's extinguishing, green shoots of new growth had already sprouted.

Pass over the saddle at 1.5 miles, returning to the west flank of Heavens Gate Ridge. Admire the impressive Sheep Creek drainage, Dry Diggins Lookout, and the Oregon Wallowas—a countryside of spectacular relief and contrast. The long line of the Boise Trail stretches north.

Steadily descend while overlooking the Snake River Canyon. The steep grassland slopes would be declared cliffs, were they but rock. By 1.8 miles, over-the-shoulder views present Seven Devils, with the best image coming at 2.3 miles where the chiseled drainage of East Fork Sheep Creek occupies the foreground.

At 2.5 miles, pass an inconspicuous trail sign tagged to a whitebark pine. The sign indicates that the Boise Trail leads south to Heavens

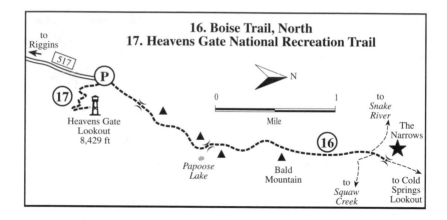

Gate Lookout and Seven Devils Station and north to Cold Springs Lookout. Beginning at 3 miles, basalt outcrops punctuate the downhill slope.

Where forest claims the slope at 3.5 miles, a primary trail angles downhill to the Snake River; proceed forward on the Boise Trail, finding the accompanying weathered trail post in 150 feet. The peculiar off-set placement owes to the sign serving double-duty, guiding travelers descending from a second undetectable trail on the slope above the Boise Trail.

At 3.6 miles reach The Narrows, the selected turnaround. Here the Boise Trail hooks right to enter the head of an eastern canyon before descending more dramatically. A silvered post marks The Narrows. Below the wooden marker, tilted, platy schistose rock shapes an intriguing toothy ridge. Views sweep north and east with looks out Squaw Creek drainage.

Hikers proceeding on the trail will find extensive burn between The Narrows and Cold Spring, which is the legacy of the Sheep Creek Fire of 1996.

17 HEAVENS GATE NATIONAL RECREATION TRAIL

Round trip: 0.6 mile
High point: 8,429 feet
Elevation change: 400 feet
Managed by: Hells Canyon National Recreation Area, Riggins
Map: USFS Hells Canyon National Recreation Area

This short tour twists to Heavens Gate Lookout and a spectacular four-state vista. Discover the Snake, Salmon, and Rapid River drainages, find exciting looks at Idaho's ghoulish Seven Devils high peak chain, and admire the Oregon Wallowas, some 50 miles distant. Eastern panoramas include Nez Perce and Payette national forests and Gospel Hump Wilderness. The best views of Seven Devils and Hells Canyon are secured in the morning.

To reach Heavens Gate from Riggins, drive south on US 95 for 1.3 miles and turn right on improved-surface Squaw Creek Road heading for Seven Devils Campground (no camp trailers or recreational vehicles). In 1.6 miles bear left, and in another 7.4 miles, turn right on Seven Devils Road/FR 517, following the signs. Typically this road opens for travel in early to mid-July.

FR 517 grows rough but remains passable for passenger vehicles with good clearance and reliable tires. In 7 miles reach the Windy Saddle junction, and bear right for Heavens Gate Vista to reach parking in 1.6 miles. There is no water at the trailhead.

Heaven's Gate Lookout

Ascend from the southern end of the parking area on a switchbacking gravel trail to tour an attractive alpine meadow slope. Wind tortured whitebark pine and high-elevation fir dot the meadow, interspersed by picturesque silvered snags. Aster, lupine, and Indian paintbrush decorate the meadow, with Jacob's ladder beneath the trees.

There is limited shade as the trail winds skyward. At this high elevation, clear days herald exceptionally blue skies. At 0.2 mile, bypass an intriguing old whitebark pine with a dead central trunk and living side trunks.

Rock jumbles and outcrops claim the upper ridge. Pikas scamper between the rocks while nutcrackers speak in raucous notes. Cross over the summit ridge, rounding to the lookout via the eastern slope. Overlook the Bridge and Cannon Creek drainages and Cannonball Mountain.

The lookout unfolds a full 360-degree view, spanning much of Idaho, with northeast Oregon, southeast Washington, and the merest hint of western Montana. Locator panels pointing out key landmarks ring the single-story tower. View not only the deepest river canyon in North America—the Snake River Canyon (Hells Canyon)—but also the second deepest canyon, Idaho's Salmon River.

Although visitors may climb to the catwalk when the lookout is staffed, the view from the rocky summit provides ample reward.

18 DRY DIGGINS LOOKOUT HIKE

Round trip: 18 miles
High point: 7,828 feet
Elevation change: 1,200 feet
Managed by: Hells Canyon National Recreation Area, Riggins
Map: USFS Hells Canyon National Recreation Area

This hike shares its initial 6.2 miles with Sheep Lake Hike (Hike 19). Find a dramatic up-and-down wilderness tour, tagging vista points and tree-filled drainages. Overlook the chiseled canyons of Sheep Creek, admire individual peaks of the Seven Devils, pause beside a waterfall, and pass time at postcard-pretty Bernard Lakes before climbing to Dry Diggins Lookout. The interior outpost holds an exceptional Hells Canyon panorama where eyes trace down an extraordinary 6,500-foot vertical relief to the bending Snake River.

To reach Dry Diggins Lookout Hike from Riggins, drive south on US

Seven Devils

95 for 1.3 miles and turn right on improved-surface Squaw Creek Road for Seven Devils Campground; camp trailers and recreational vehicles are not permitted. In 1.6 miles bear left, and in another 7.4 miles, turn right on Seven Devils Road/FR 517, which usually opens for travel in early to mid-July. While rough, the road remains passable for passenger vehicles with good clearance. In 7 miles, reach Windy Saddle and bear left for trailhead parking in 0.1 mile. There is no water at the trailhead or campgrounds.

On the marked Seven Devils Trail (Trail 124), pass behind the restroom, round the head of a gulch, and skirt Windy Saddle Campground to enter Hells Canyon Wilderness at 0.1 mile; horseback riders arrive on the right. The wide, well-graded trail descends and switchbacks amid an open-cathedral forest of lodgepole pine and fir. At 0.5 mile, come upon the first of a pair of spurs branching to a stock-watering site.

Meadow openings present the immediate stony peaks. At 0.7 mile, pass a marked trail to the Snake River. From 1.7 to 2.2 miles, prolonged switchbacks ascend through forest, topping Middle Ridge for exceptional views of the east fork and west fork Sheep Creek drainages, Heavens Gate Ridge, and Dry Diggins Lookout.

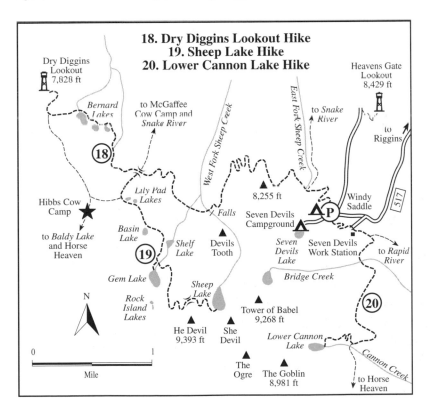

75

By 2.7 miles the trail is both steep and switchbacking as it descends into the West Fork Sheep Creek drainage. He Devil, She Devil, Devils Tooth, and several unnamed peaks and crags rise at the canyon head. Where the trail traverses an extensive talus slope at 3.4 miles the path is remarkably rock-free.

With a meandering descent through fir-spruce forest, cross the West Fork Sheep Creek below a divided, white-rushing 15-foot falls. The crossing is accomplished via logs or wading.

Cross a pair of side streams via stepping stones or wading, then switchback uphill, traversing a boulder-talus slope and past burn. Find more great views of the devilish line-up at the head of Sheep Creek.

At 6.2 miles claim the saddle junction where hikers split off to Dry Diggins Lookout or Sheep Lake, among other destinations. For hikers wishing to visit both the lookout and Sheep Lake, tent-sized flats may be found on the saddle, but water must be obtained elsewhere.

Forgo the first right to McGaffee Cow Camp (Trail 140); instead take the second right (Trail 57) for Dry Diggins Lookout. Watch for signs. The trail continues to weave through a burn with both living and singed trees. Wildflowers, dwarf huckleberry, black twinberry, and other low shrubs interweave forest and outcrop. Next comes a series of fairly steep downhill switchbacks that are accompanied by views of the destination tower.

With the flattening of the trail (6.8 miles), leave behind the burn and soon hear gurgling headwaters. By the crossing at 7 miles though, the creek may be dry. After a third crossing, switchback uphill to reach the first Bernard Lake, a small shallow water rimmed by spruce and lodgepole pine. Catch another look at He Devil and She Devil as the trail rounds away from the pond and its false hellebore bog.

Where the trail next flattens, detour 50 feet right to peer out a canyon gouge to Cottonwood Butte. By 7.7 miles round the next Bernard Lake, which is a bigger and deeper crescent in a forested basin overshadowed by exposed rock peaks and rims.

At 8 miles reach the third and largest Bernard Lake, an expansive oval platter at the base of the lookout's ridge. Outcrops along the opposite shore shape deeper holes; lily pads adorn the shallows. Next skirt a circular cow-lily pond, cross the outlet, and bear right for a switchbacked ascent.

Travel an exposed rocky slope with balsamroot, ground juniper, and phlox. In a high meadow at 8.5 miles, come upon a marked junction. Go right for Dry Diggins Lookout, passing through high meadows and pocket forests; Trail 56 heads left for Hibbs Cow Camp.

Views of the immediate alpine extend little clue that this is Hells Canyon country. Find confirmation with a dizzying downward look to the Snake River as the trail hooks left at 8.7 miles. Morning lighting best displays the creased canyon walls, benches, and arid steppes.

Travel over outcrop to reach the two-story lookout (9 miles); touring its catwalk unfolds the 360-degree view. For a fine cap to the tour, views include Hat Point, the Wallowas, Granite Creek drainage, Bernard Lakes, a partial lineup of the Seven Devils, the peaks of Six Lakes Basin, Heavens Gate Ridge, and the glistening Snake River.

Sheep Lake

19   SHEEP LAKE HIKE

Round trip: 20.5 miles, with lake side-trips
High point: 8,300 feet
Elevation change: 1,700 feet
Managed by: Hells Canyon National Recreation Area, Riggins
Map: USFS Hells Canyon National Recreation Area

This hike shares its initial 6.2 miles with Dry Diggins Lookout Hike (Hike 18, see map p. 75). Rewards for this wilderness challenge include exceptional Hells Canyon–Seven Devils vistas, hopscotch travel lake-to-lake, and a spectacular climax where the indigo waters of Sheep Lake are cradled in the lap of the Seven Devils. Each of the trail's lakes has potential campsites that meet wilderness parameters.

To reach the trailhead of the Sheep Lake Hike from Riggins, drive south on US 95 for 1.3 miles and turn right on improved-surface Squaw Creek Road for Seven Devils Campground (no trailers or recreational vehicles). In 1.6 miles bear left, and in another 7.4 miles, turn

Butterfly on asters

right on Seven Devils Road/FR 517, which usually opens early to mid-July. While rock-studded, FR 517 remains passable for most passenger vehicles; go slow. At Windy Saddle in 7 miles, bear left for trailhead parking in 0.1 mile. Water is not available at the trailhead or campgrounds.

Depart Windy Saddle on the wide, well-graded Seven Devils Trail (Trail 124) for an up-and-down trek through Hells Canyon Wilderness, dipping to drainages and attaining vista points. In the first mile, bypass spurs to stock-watering sites and the sign-marked trail to the Snake River. Alternately travel forest and meadow, attaining the first big vista at 2.2 miles atop a jut isolating the east and west forks of Sheep Creek.

Enjoy views of He Devil and She Devil, as well as Devils Tooth, as the trail descends a series of switchbacks to the West Fork Sheep Creek crossing (4.5 miles). A 15-foot waterfall just upstream from the log crossing (or fording) is an ideal place to pause.

After a pair of side-stream crossings, switchbacks then scale a talus slope and recovering burn to reach the saddle junction at 6.2 miles. For greater detail on this 6.2-mile stretch, refer to the Dry Diggins Lookout Hike (Hike 18).

Top the saddle and bear left for Seven Devils Trail proceeding toward Hibbs Cow Camp and Little Granite Creek. Avoid the right-branching trails to McGaffee Cow Camp (Trail 140) and Dry Diggins Lookout (Trail 57). With a meandering climb, travel a broad summit flat—a tapestry of barren openings, lush meadows, and snag-woven alpine forests. Follow the tracked path and steer away from a gravelly channel to reach a fork at 6.6 miles. Here turn left per the unobtrusive "Sheep Lake" sign; this is Trail 123.

Pass Lily Pad Lake, a dark circular water ringed by lily pads and a rim of golden grasses with the Seven Devils as a backdrop. A series of trodden paths arise in the area; bear left to edge a picturesque high meadow below unnamed peaks.

Cross the meadow spring and enter a cool alpine forest unscathed by fire. Rocks to the left of the trail overlook Sheep Creek drainage. At 7.4 miles bear left for the main trail; spurs to the right lead to Basin Lake.

Detour to view this beautiful, deep green lake in a regal high peaks basin. Trout gracefully part the water. Hawk, deer, nutcracker, and pika number among the other wildlife sightings.

A switchbacking ascent leads to Shelf Lake, which is the next lake basin. The trail rounds above this second temptress nestled below a toothy ridge. At its far end, find developed lake-access trails. Alternately pass from sun to shade.

At 8.2 miles the trail forks. Follow Gem Lake outlet upstream for 0.1 mile to view this deep secluded lake in the shadow of He Devil, or cross the outlet to continue the tour to Sheep Lake.

En route to Sheep Lake, the ascent resumes, drawing deeper into the rocky realm. Lichens color the dark rock jumbles and cliffs; phlox, gentian, heather, and ground juniper spot the harsh landscape. At 8.6 miles, glimpse the bladder-shaped blue water of the now distant Gem Lake. Rock Island Lakes elude scrutiny, requiring off-trail travel for a view or visit.

From the broad saddle overlooking Sheep Lake (9.2 miles), switchbacks descend to the shore of this indigo beauty (10 miles). A magnificent steep-sided rocky bowl, irregular shoreline, aquamarine shallows, and tree, rock, and alpine shores contribute to Sheep Lake's memorable character. Pocked and scalloped snowfields decorate the ridge. View the Tower of Babel, She Devil, and He Devil. Rocky peninsulas suggest admiring, fishing, or a polar-bear dip.

20 LOWER CANNON LAKE HIKE

Round trip: 8 miles
High point: 7,500 feet
Elevation change: 800 feet
Managed by: Hells Canyon National Recreation Area, Riggins
Map: USFS Hells Canyon National Recreation Area

This hike follows part of the historic Boise Trail, an early-day north-south transportation route that opened up western Idaho to exploration and settlement (see map p. 75). The rolling trail passes through forest, high meadow, and burn habitats, and offers views out Cannon and Bridge Creek drainages. Lower Cannon Lake, a crystalline lake in a high peak basin, puts a sterling cap on the journey.

From Riggins, drive south on US 95 for 1.3 miles and turn right on improved-surface Squaw Creek Road for Seven Devils Campground (no camp trailers or recreational vehicles). In 1.6 miles bear left, and in another 7.4 miles, turn right on Seven Devils Road/FR 517, which usually opens in early to mid-July. While rock-studded, FR 517 remains passable for most passenger vehicles with good tires. Reach Windy Saddle in 7 miles and bear left to find trailhead parking in 0.1 mile. Water is not available at the trailhead or campgrounds.

Head south on the marked Boise Trail (Trail 101), opposite Windy

Lower Cannon Lake

Saddle trailhead parking. Wonderful views engage from the start: admire the nearby high rocky peak marked by deep creases, thin tree lines, and snowy shadows. Be sure to watch for moving snowfields, which are actually mountain goats.

The trail swings left across a meadow slope, overlooking the Bridge Creek and Rapid River drainages. Bunchgrasses, aster, lupine, and cinquefoil, with solitaire and clustered whitebark and lodgepole pines, dress the slope. The trail is wide, switchbacked, and well-maintained.

At 0.2 mile pass through and resecure a gate. Ahead, watch for trail signs that point hikers around a pack station, over a dirt forest road, and past Seven Devils Work Station.

Alternately travel meadow and forest with firs joining the pines. Cannonball Mountain below seemingly erupts out of Cannon Creek. At 0.75 mile pass through a rustic lodgepole gate to enter Hells Canyon Wilderness. Avoid the Silvers Trail, which heads left to Rapid River.

Descend steadily alongside a small ravine until the trail briefly emerges in a dry meadow, where there is a clear view of the Tower of Babel. At 1.6 miles, cross Bridge Creek via hewn log, rocks, or fording. Afterward the trail flattens, touring fire-culled forest. The Rapid River Fire of 1994 swept portions of the trail, leaving snags amid the living trees.

The trail next contours the folded headwall slope of Bridge Creek. Where it rounds a point at 3 miles, return to unscathed mature forest, where squirrels busily knock down seed cones in late summer. Elsewhere, the burn habitat reclaims the tour.

At 3.2 miles, come to a marked trail junction opposite a humped outcrop that offers a drainage overlook thanks to the fire. The Boise Trail proceeds forward from the junction; bear right to reach (Lower) Cannon Lake.

The lake trail, Trail 126, switchbacks up an arid wildflower and outcrop slope with blackened snags and passes into a basin at 3.4 miles. Pearly everlasting adorns the sides of the rolling trail. Cross Cannon Creek via silver logs, and in 0.4 mile, reach the wetland shore of Cannon Lake.

Silver snags, spired high-elevation trees, and crags create a ragged skyline for this sparkling orb. In places talus and strewn logs shape the shore instead of the wetland meadow. Dragonflies, dipper, and fish divert attention; pikas favor the talus slope. On the lake's left side find shade and a few appropriate camp flats.

21 WEST FORK RAPID RIVER TRAIL

Round trip: 9.5 miles (to West Fork Bridge)
High point: 3,400 feet
Elevation change: 1,100 feet
Managed by: Salmon River Ranger District, Nez Perce National Forest
Maps: USFS Nez Perce National Forest, USFS Payette National Forest, USFS Hells Canyon National Recreation Area

In an isolated part of Hells Canyon National Recreation Area, this rolling tour hugs and crisscrosses the Rapid Wild and Scenic River, pursuing the waterway upstream to its west fork. On the first-rate tour, catch spellbinding looks at the racing river as it flows clear, cold, and deep. A scattering of trees adorn the north-facing slopes while grasslands mantle those facing south. Sheer cliffs, black hollows, deep creases, and overhangs bring added interest to the river corridor.

To reach the trail, go 4 miles south of Riggins on US 95 and turn west on Rapid River Road toward Rapid River Fish Hatchery. In 2.4 miles find the signed trailhead (Trail 113) on the right; the entrance to the Idaho Power-owned hatchery is on the left. With roadside parking for only a handful of vehicles, be courteous when pulling in to allow others access. Day hikers may find parking at the hatchery between 8:00 A.M. and 5:00 P.M.; restrooms, water, and picnic tables are also available. Avoid posted areas.

On the north side of the river ascend an old jeep trail, hiking upstream through Idaho Power land; be sure to resecure the hiker gate upon passing. A well-marked, well-cut foot trail proceeds through the tight canyon. Hike 100 feet above the river to enter national forest land in 0.25 mile. Mountain mahogany lends its signature shape to the slope above the trail while mixed grasses, clover, and a succession of wildflowers vegetate the slope.

Upstream, a conical peak to the south and a bulging northern cliff shape a memorable canyon gateway. At an unmarked fork at 0.6 mile, keep to the main trail rounding the slope; avoid the one angling uphill.

The shadeless tour vacillates between 50 and 100 feet above the river. The canyon slope shows three tiers: the immediate rock shaping the river channel, the grassy mid-slope holding the trail, and the striking cliff rim. Ocean spray, clematis, larkspur, Oregon grape, wallflower, and desert parsley variously decorate the slope.

Below, the river twists between natural banks, spilling over cobble and around rocks. At 1.1 miles, reach river level and cross the first bridge. Upstream the river has gorge-like drama; downstream the serene water is framed by leafy shores.

Remain close to the river for much of the next mile. Kingfisher, dipper, songbird, and merganser enjoy distinct niches. Watch for elk and deer on the slopes. By 2.3 miles, fir and yew shade the tour.

Again draw above the Rapid River, traversing grassland and scree. Upon returning to the river, bypass a camp flat at 3.5 miles. In general, this steep-walled, narrow canyon limits overnight possibilities. Upstream from the 4-mile mark the river is more turbulent, spilling around and between rocks.

Rapid River

82

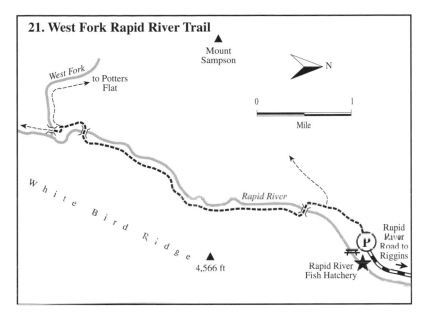

21. West Fork Rapid River Trail

Mount Sampson

West Fork

to Potters Flat

N

0   1

Mile

White Bird Ridge

Rapid River

4,566 ft

P

Rapid River Road to Riggins

Rapid River Fish Hatchery

Next, cross back over Rapid River for a fairly steep ascent, drawing 200 feet above the waterway. At 4.5 miles come to a marked junction and exceptional canyon overview, where a jut along the north slope shapes a Rapid River bend and frames the side canyon of the West Fork.

The path straight ahead continues the West Fork Rapid River Trail to Potters Flat. To end this hike at the West Fork bridge (4.75 miles) bear left, descending the nose of the ridge via the Rapid River Trail (Trail 59). Both river trails invite further exploration. Hikers should avoid building campfires within this special riparian corridor, and be alert for rattlesnakes and poison ivy.

22 KINNEY CREEK TRAIL

Round trip: 7.2 miles (to the first saddle)
High point: 3,500 feet
Elevation change: 1,800 feet
Managed by: Council Ranger District or Weiser Ranger District,
    Payette National Forest
Maps: USFS Payette National Forest, USFS Hells Canyon National
    Recreation Area

Exploring the east wall of Hells Canyon, this breath-stealing trail (Trail 221) presents stunning landscapes of bold, imposing cliffs, steep grass-and-scree slope, pocket forests, and the broad Snake River.

Travel up the steep rocky side canyon of Kinney Creek before contouring the front wall southward.

Spring finds the trail at its finest and holds the best opportunity for wildlife viewing: chukar and grouse commonly startle hikers, and sightings of deer, elk, bear, mountain goat, bighorn sheep, eagle, and peregrine falcon are all possible. Despite annual maintenance, portions of the trail can disappear in the grassland. Scan the slope ahead for clues, and watch for cairns. Also, watch footing throughout, as steep grades and loose rocks can easily up-end hikers.

To reach Kinney Creek Trail from Halfway, Oregon, drive east on OR 86 for 16 miles, proceed across the Snake River bridge into Idaho, and bear left, heading north toward Hells Canyon Dam on FR 454, the east shore road. From Idaho, reach the east shore road 40 miles northwest of Cambridge via ID 71. In 6 miles, pass Idaho Power's Hells Canyon Park, where drinking water is available. After 8.8 miles more, park on the south shore of Kinney Creek. Find the marked trailhead on the north shore.

Hike east skirting the bay pond at the mouth of Kinney Creek, touring its rugged gulch amphitheater. Horsetail reeds and mullein adorn the banks. Cross-creek views feature the cliffs, crags, and forest of the opposite canyon wall. Loose scree at times claims the trailbed; beware of poison ivy growing in the rock.

A nonpoisonous hog-nosed snake

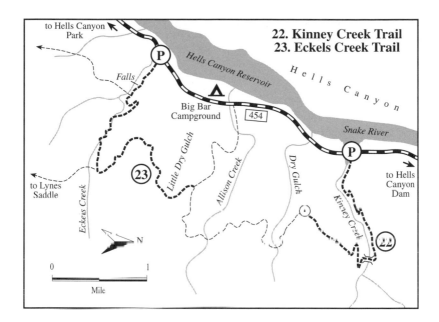

to Hells Canyon
Park

22. Kinney Creek Trail
23. Eckels Creek Trail

Find the first set of switchbacks at 0.5 mile. Where the switchbacks halt, an over-the-shoulder glance offers a Snake River-Hells Canyon view. Continue hiking through scree or desert parsley and grassland slopes.

By 1 mile, reach the heart of the cliff country enfolding Kinney Creek and its banner of leafy shrubs, waterleaf, nettles, and horsetail reeds. Where the trail passes closer to Kinney Creek, greenery may overwhelm the path, but the line of travel remains apparent.

At 1.8 miles cross the footbridge over Kinney Creek now on Trail 222, and proceed upstream for 0.1 mile. (Trail 221, undefined and in need of reconstruction, continues up Grassy Ridge.) Next bear right to follow switchbacks uphill, avoiding a secondary path that continues upstream. With the steep ascent, enjoy fine looks at Kinney Creek curving out its canyon, the textured terrain, and the canyon-"V" framing a West Rim view.

The switchbacks end at 2.6 miles where a steep uphill assault begins. Emerge from Kinney Creek drainage, topping the grassy saddle destination parting Kinney Creek and Dry Gulch, 3.6 miles. The saddle sweeps west to an outcrop point that serves up a rewarding final view.

Hikers wishing to continue the front-wall tour should bear left upon reaching the saddle and keep a sharp eye out for a low cairn in the deep grasses. Visually track the line of the trail as it contours south to fill in the trail gaps. Trail 222 journeys south to meet Allison Creek Trail (Trail 514) and later Eckels Creek Trail (Trail 223, Hike 23), both of which offer loop-travel options; consult a map.

23 ECKELS CREEK TRAIL

Round trip: 10.8 miles (to Allison Creek Trail)
High point: 3,800 feet
Elevation change: 2,080 feet
Managed by: Council Ranger District or Weiser Ranger District,
**   Payette National Forest**
Maps: USFS Payette National Forest, USFS Hells Canyon National
**   Recreation Area**

Despite annual maintenance, this rugged trail remains faint in places, with skidding gravel stealing footing, but it quickly provides stirring Hells Canyon–Snake River overviews. Springtime finds the grassland resplendent in wildflowers. Wildlife encounters may include deer, elk, bear, hawk, vulture, hog-nosed snake, and rattlesnake.

Although geographically close to Kinney Creek Trail (Hike 22 see map p. 85), each has its own signature. Along Eckels Creek Trail, be dazzled by bald grassland slopes, steep relief, folded side canyons, and cascading Eckels Creek.

From Halfway, Oregon, drive east on OR 86 for 16 miles, proceed across the Snake River bridge into Idaho, and bear left, heading north toward Hells Canyon Dam on FR 454. From Idaho, reach FR 454 40 miles northwest of Cambridge via ID 71. Water is available in 6 miles at Idaho Power's Hells Canyon Park. Drive 6.5 miles past the park to

Deer

Eckels Creek Canyon

find the signed Eckels Creek Trail (Trail 223) on the right; parking is on the left.

Hike east touring below an impressive rocky crest to the north. First travel a matted-grass track, then a narrow, rocky footpath for a moderate-to-steep ascent. Eckels Creek threads below the trail to the south, its tree-and-shrub ribbon parting desert slopes. To the west, view the stern Oregon rim.

Sumac, phlox, balsamroot, desert parsley, and showings of poison ivy dress the trail's sides. By 0.5 mile, encounter more outcrops. A falls seasonally decorates the creek course; look for the folding together of its white streamers amid a rush of greenery below twin pines. Wild rose, paintbrush, larkspur, and hyacinth expand the color spectrum. Mountain mahogany dots the rock ledges.

At 0.75 mile the canyon-"V" frames a fine Snake River-West Rim view. Where hikers come upon a trail stake and turn left, another cascade adorns Eckels Creek. The Hells Canyon terrain remains striking, with its sheer relief, tiered pyramid cliffs, and steeple-topped conifers.

Round above the left headwater fork of Eckels Creek and enter an area of leafy trees and shrubs. Here find the first shade and a sometimes brushing passage (1.2 miles). Switchback in and out of the drainage, crisscrossing the creek. Early in the year expect to wade; later, rocks provide dry footing.

Leave the drainage, topping an outcrop point with a lone pine and fir (1.8 miles), for a grand look back at the accomplishment. Where the trail switchbacks to the right at 2 miles, another viewpoint adds looks east toward the Horse Mountain–Lynes Saddle area. Both vantages offer satisfactory endings, should hikers wish to shorten the hike.

The trail now contours ever higher, rounding to the back side of the northern hill. Reach a junction stake at 2.6 miles. Here leave the Eckels Creek Trail (Trail 223), which proceeds forward to Lynes Saddle but is largely undefined and in need of reconstruction. Instead follow Trail 222 left to return to the front wall, which is the east wall of Hells Canyon.

Initially contour the upper slope of Eckels Creek Canyon, overlooking the hike's start. Although the trail keeps a steady line, elk and horse hooves have ruptured the bed. By 3.4 miles round onto the front wall, again viewing the Snake River and West Rim.

The next shade can be found amid a mature pine grove at 3.9 miles. In early spring, avalanche lily decorates the stand; arnica waits in the wings. While plodding through the side canyon folds, one learns how deceptive distance can be in this terrain.

At 4.75 miles, cross Little Dry Gulch. Along the next point, the trail fades but cairns offer guidance. At 5.4 miles top a grassy side ridge to find exceptional views and the junction stake marking the turnaround or a decision point for loop travel.

For a long loop (15.4 miles), bear right and continue the front-wall tour to Kinney Creek, a grueling long-distance trek. For the short loop (8-plus miles), turn left to make a sharp descent along the Allison Creek Trail (Trail 514); expect some wading and watch footing. Both loops require road travel along FR 454; turn left (south) upon meeting the road.

OREGON WALLOWAS, EAGLE CAP
WILDERNESS NORTH

Chimney Lake

2A BEAR CREEK TRAIL

Round trip: 10.5 miles (to Bear Creek Guard Station)
High point: 4,600 feet
Elevation change: 750 feet
**Managed by: Eagle Cap Ranger District, Wallowa-Whitman National
  Forest**
**Maps: USFS Wallowa-Whitman National Forest, Imus Geographics
  Wallowa Mountains Eagle Cap Wilderness**

This hike (Trail 1653) parallels Bear Creek upstream, offering pleasing creek overlooks and limited access. The sparkling Bear Creek waters, mid-elevation forests, wildflowers and wildlife, and the ease of the trail all recommend a tour. Rustic Bear Creek Guard Station, occupying a broad creek flat, signals a convenient turnaround for day hikers and may suggest an overnight stay to backpackers.

On the west side of the town of Wallowa where OR 82 enters a 90-degree bend, go west on First Street at the sign for Bear Creek. In 0.4 mile, turn left (south) on Bear Creek Road. The surface eventually changes to dirt, with areas of coarse gravel. Upon entering the national forest in 5.6 miles, the road name changes to Little Bear Saddle Road/FR 8250. At the junction of FR 8250 and FR 8250.040 in another 1.2 miles, proceed straight on FR 8250.040 for Boundary Campground and Bear Creek Trailhead. The large trail parking area is 0.9 mile from the junction.

Hike a closed jeep trail south along Bear Creek, touring a fir-spruce forest intermixed with larch and ponderosa pine. The lane soon tapers to trail width. The beauty of Bear Creek is displayed in its riffles, deep, clear pools, and stands of alder and currant. At 0.25 mile, cross a horse bridge over Bear Creek. The trail remains about 3-feet

Bear Creek

wide and is well-used by hikers and horseback riders. Arnica, lupine, wood violet, twinflower, and Oregon grape weave the forest mat.

A tight forest of 6- to 12-inch-diameter trees enfolds the tour prior to the ascent at 1 mile, where outcrop walls force the trail to a higher contour. Up-canyon views feature Fox Point. On the bluffs, find desert parsley and shooting stars. Boulders accent the creek 100 feet below. In another 0.5 mile, travel a forest flat alongside Bear Creek.

Where the trail next rolls away, cross Baker Gulch via rocks and gravel. Elk tracks intermix with the horse-hoof prints as the trail remains above and away from the creek. By 2.5 miles Goat Mountain is visible.

Return creekside at 3.5 miles, alternately touring bench or forested flat, which is home to a few campsites. Where meadow slopes open up the canyon, gain new perspectives on Fox Point and its rocky shoulder. Beyond the meadow, looks left present the craggy skyline of Huckleberry Mountain.

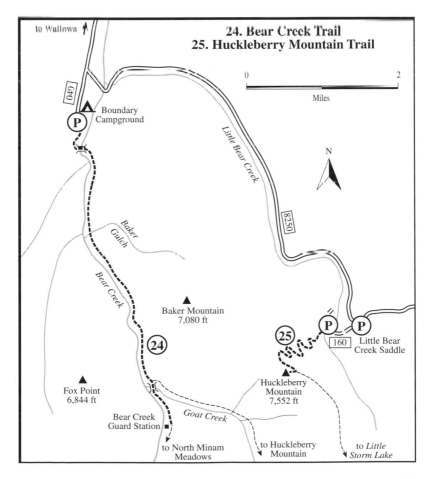

Enter Eagle Cap Wilderness (4.1 miles) to encounter a forest of lodgepole pine, where winter downfalls plague spring trail crews. Hikers getting a jump on the season may find a steeplechase of the spiny pines.

At a clearing at 4.7 miles, come to the signed junction with the Goat Creek Trail (Trail 1665); this secondary-looking trail heads left upstream along Goat Creek. Proceed forward crossing the Goat Creek bridge to continue the Bear Creek Trail. At the junction clearing, admire the three peaks that shape the area's character: Fox Point, Goat Mountain, and Huckleberry Mountain.

At 5.2 miles, a spur branches right, leading to the destination guard station—a scenic cabin amid an open flat. Bear Creek Trail continues deeper into the wilderness. Large hewn-log beams and caulked seams fashion the cabin; its covered porch offers shelter from raindrops or shade from sun. Behind the cabin, Bear Creek courses between open gravel bars.

25   HUCKLEBERRY MOUNTAIN TRAIL

Round trip: 3.6 miles (4.6 miles, if the gate is closed)
High point: 7,551 feet
Elevation change: 1,950 feet
Managed by: Eagle Cap Ranger District, Wallowa-Whitman National Forest
Maps: USFS Wallowa-Whitman National Forest, Imus Geographics Wallowa Mountains Eagle Cap Wilderness

This short, rigorous ascent delivers hikers to a lofty Wallowa Mountain post for a superb 360-degree panoramic view, encompassing the high peaks, Wallowa Valley, and Hells Canyon (see map p. 91). En route, assemble the puzzle pieces of the panorama: travel both mid- and high-elevation forests, cross meadow slopes, and find alpine flora, tortured trees, and clues to a past lookout tower atop Huckleberry Mountain.

On the west side of the town of Wallowa where OR 82 enters a 90-degree bend, go west on First Street at the sign for Bear Creek. In 0.4 mile, turn left on Bear Creek Road. The surface soon changes to dirt with areas of coarse gravel. Upon entering the national forest in 5.6 miles, the road name changes to Little Bear Saddle Road/FR 8250.

In another 1.2 miles, bear left remaining on FR 8250, now a high-clearance vehicle road that is unsuitable for passenger vehicles. At the fork in 3.7 miles again bear left. In another 3.1 miles, turn right on FR 8250.160; look for a weathered trail sign on a tree to the right. Find parking at the corner when FR 8250.160 is gated (June 1 through September 16). When the gate is open, proceed on FR 8250.160 for 0.5 mile. Pull-in parking for two vehicles is available upon crossing Little Bear Creek.

Huckleberry Mountain summit

The unmarked Huckleberry Mountain Trail (Trail 1667) heads up-stream from the parking turnout at Little Bear Creek. Travel a mature forest of fir, larch, and spruce, with huckleberry and meadow rue. Be-fore long, the 3-foot-wide churned rocky forest trail ascends a meadow swath. Where the path forks (0.2 mile), proceed straight up the slope. An unofficial trail heads left.

The mountain trail narrows, enters shallow "S" curves, and then switchbacks. Looks north present the Wallowa Valley tapestry. Travel alternates between forest and meadow. Before long, northeast views span the grassland expanse to Hells Canyon and Idaho's Seven Devils; looks northwest strain to the Wenaha-Tucannon Wilderness—ample reward for 0.5 mile of puffing.

When budget restrictions prevent annual trail maintenance, expect a couple of troubling downfalls and some erosion. Balsamroot colors the upper slopes while lodgepole pine, spruce, and larch alter the forest mix.

As mountain hemlock and whitebark pine signal a transition into alpine habitat, alternating switchbacks offer glimpses at the summit plateau of Huckleberry Mountain. At the next meadow crossing, find a 180-degree northern view.

Next, charge uphill alongside a steep side drainage, and cross where it flattens. Here a wider trail parts a lodgepole pine forest as the as-cent loses some of its steepness. With a switchback, contour to the top of the ridge to reach the Eagle Cap Wilderness sign at 1.6 miles. An off-trail detour offers vistas south and west at Goat and Bear Creek drainages.

Hike past the sign through alpine meadows of heather, dwarf

huckleberry, and pearly everlasting, with patches of false hellebore. The trail then angles up the north flank of Huckleberry Mountain, topping the rocky grassland of the summit plateau (1.75 miles). Look for a side trail switchbacking right; it leads to the former lookout site. The main trail, barely discernible, proceeds straight along the summit ridge.

The lookout post pulls together all previous views and to the east adds the snowy peaks above the Lostine River. A ring of rocks marks the former tower location, as do rusting tin, splintering wood, old stove plates, and fragments of wire. Do not disturb the artifacts, which are all part of the mountain's legacy. Winds can punish the summit.

26   HUNTER FALLS TRAIL

Round trip: 0.6 mile
High point: 5,100 feet
Elevation change: 200 feet
Managed by: Eagle Cap Ranger District, Wallowa-Whitman National Forest
Map: USFS Wallowa-Whitman National Forest

This simple leg-stretcher (Trail 1829) takes travelers to a sheltered waterfall on Lake Creek, where the creek speeds to join the Lostine River. Boulders deposited high along the canyon's sides reveal that here the glacial ice once stood 1,500 feet thick.

To reach Hunter Falls Trail from OR 82 in Lostine (west of Enterprise), go south on Lostine River Road/FR 8210, a paved and improved-surface road. In 11.5 miles, the trailhead is on the left, just north of Lake Creek. What remains of a trail-post cairn marks the falls trail. There is parking for a couple of vehicles at the trailhead; additional parking is at the guard station 100 yards farther south.

Begin with a steep burst of climb through a relatively open lodgepole pine forest to reach a small ridge above Lake Creek where alders interweave the woods and hikers find a fine creek overlook. Here the trail swings left away from the creek. At the fork at 0.1 mile, bear left along the lower rock-lined path. Traverse a small meadow and rimming forest of fir, western larch, and ponderosa pine. Lush grasses, snowberry, yarrow, Indian paintbrush, and buckwheat contribute to the ground cover.

As the trail again tours above rushing Lake Creek, find cottonwood, alder, maple, and dogwood. The granite boulders of the creek shape 1-foot-high cascades.

At 0.25 mile, the trail splits. Hike downhill 50 feet for a base-view of the broad 30- to 40-foot falls; be careful on the pitched sandy descent. Wading provides a square-on view, but chill waters sting the feet.

Proceed upstream and with a steep 100-foot charge, view the upper falls. Although the trail continues, it grows more and more faint. Even on this short tour, hikers may spy mule deer, hawk, or flicker.

Hunter Falls

27 CHIMNEY LAKE HIKE

Round trip: 10 miles
High point: 7,600 feet
Elevation change: 2,500 feet
Managed by: Eagle Cap Ranger District, Wallowa-Whitman National Forest
Maps: USFS Wallowa-Whitman National Forest, Imus Geographics Wallowa Mountains Eagle Cap Wilderness

This wilderness hike begins on the popular Bowman Trail (Trail 1651) and zigzags up the west wall of the Lostine River drainage. Collect views of Marble Point and Eagle Cap, gaze down at the tinsel-like Lostine River, tour picturesque Brownie Basin, and visit tranquil Laverty Lakes before reaching the shining beauty of Chimney Lake. There is ample invitation for outward exploration with Hobo, Wood, and John Henry lakes. Eastern brook trout provide sport for fishermen.

To reach the trailhead for the Chimney Lake Hike from OR 82 in Lostine, drive 14.1 miles south on Lostine River Road/FR 8210, a paved and improved-surface road. Bowman Trailhead is on the right, with parking for up to ten passenger vehicles. Horse-trailer parking is 0.1 mile farther south at the Frances Lake/Bowman Trailhead.

Cross the concrete bridge overlooking the clean water of the Lostine River, with its bouldery streambed and rock ledge. Then hike upstream passing through a lodgepole pine–fir forest on the well-traveled trail.

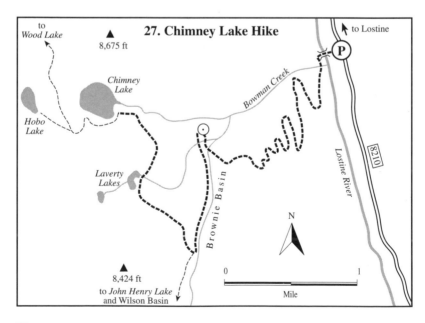

27. Chimney Lake Hike

Chimney Lake

Enter the wilderness, coming to a rock crossing (seasonal fording) of Bowman Creek. Long angling contours advance the trail for a comfortable measured ascent. Alternately tour forest and meadow, gathering views after the first switchback at 0.4 mile. At the next switchback, overlook a racing chute on Bowman Creek as it surfs over a canted cliff 50 feet long. An unnamed peak towers at the head of the creek canyon.

At 1.3 miles, enjoy funneled looks up the East Fork Lostine River drainage to Eagle Cap—a grand presentation of the famous peak. At 1.6 miles, a forested shelf below the trail holds a campsite with cross-canyon views of Marble Point. Later a fang-toothed peak captures skyline attention.

By 2.1 miles enter the "high country," with granite outcrops and cliffs, talus slopes, and fir, spruce, and whitebark pine. Next, cross the cascading water at the head forks of Bowman Creek and the outlet of Laverty Lakes. At 2.75 miles an outcrop point may waylay hikers for a breather. Glimpse Hurricane Divide and the top of Twin Peaks above the Marble Point ridge.

Cross back over the Laverty Lakes outlet to soon contour the slope overlooking the long alpine meadow of Brownie Basin (3.3 miles).

Jagged peaks, sweeping saddles, and Flagstaff Point frame the basin threaded by a shimmery stream. At the marked trail junction at 3.8 miles, turn right for Chimney Lake on Trail 1659. The forward path leads to Wilson Basin and John Henry Lake.

Ascending from Brownie Basin, cross exposed granite outcrops with rewarding Lostine River drainage views. At 4.3 miles, reach and round the main Laverty Lakes body, a serene mixed-depth mountain pool below a talus-skirted peak. To view the upper lake in the next basin requires cross-country travel up a rocky slope along the inlet stream. Pikas favor the rocky realm; ground squirrels prefer the alpine forest edge.

Cross the outlet and round toward Chimney Lake, again traveling exposed outcrop slopes dotted by spired conifers and snags. By 4.7 miles, peer through a saddle at Eagle Cap and its high-peak gallery.

At 5 miles, reach deep Chimney Lake cupped amid ragged peaks; a dark red dike streaks one wall. Steep talus slopes, alpine tree clusters, and a couple of rock islands add to the lake's charm. Nearby lie a couple of inappropriate wilderness campsites; camp no closer than 0.25 mile to this fragile lake body or to Laverty Lakes. The trail continues, rounding above and away from Chimney Lake to split off at a saddle for Hobo and Wood lakes.

28 MAXWELL LAKE TRAIL

Round trip: 8.6 miles
High point: 7,750 feet
Elevation change: 2,300 feet
Managed by: Eagle Cap Ranger District, Wallowa-Whitman National Forest
Maps: USFS Wallowa-Whitman National Forest, Imus Geographics Wallowa Mountains Eagle Cap Wilderness

This hard-climbing "Jekyll and Hyde" trail (Trail 1674) travels the western wall of the Lostine River Canyon, advancing first via measured switchbacks, then breaking into a mad all-out scramble to the lake divide. The tour unites the high-walled beauty of the Lostine River drainage and the stunning waters of Maxwell Lake, cradled in a high-mountain bowl and surrounded by chiseled granite ridges, conical peaks, and sliding rock slopes. A second smaller lake beckons a short cross-country trek. In late summer, watch pikas scurry back and forth with grasses, building their winter larders. Fishing poles earn their portage.

To reach Maxwell Lake Trail from Lostine, turn south off OR 82 at the sign for Lostine River Campgrounds. This is Lostine River Road/ FR 8210, a paved and gravel route; follow it south for 16.6 miles. The trail leaves Shady Campground at the Lostine River footbridge, but management plans call for the trailhead's relocation. Look for it.

Meanwhile, cross the bridge to enter a fir-spruce forest accented by bride's bonnet and windflower. At 0.1 mile, stepping stones ease the crossing of Maxwell Lake outlet. The zigzagging route alternately travels forest, open meadows, and shrub-mantled slopes. Alder, rocky mountain maple, nettles, false hellebore, and few quaking aspen crowd drainages.

Up-canyon views build as a few ponderosa pines interlace the forest. At 1.6 miles, cross another drainage that is usually large enough to allow for the topping of water jugs. Smaller, trickling drainages follow. Occasionally glimpse the Lostine River, glistening up from its forested canyon bottom.

By 2.5 miles, views extend up the East Fork Lostine River drainage, but the angle denies a west canyon view. On the steep flank of Hurricane Divide (Lostine's east canyon wall), a thin ribbony stream catches the eye. The forest mix changes, showing subalpine fir and lodgepole pine.

Maxwell Lake campsite

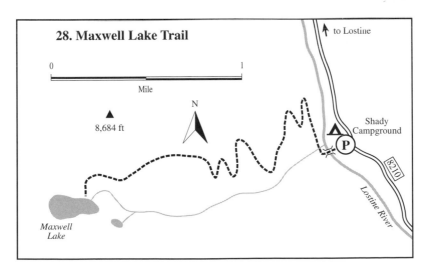

At 3 miles, the trail undergoes transformation to bring on the demanding uphill haul. Sounds of the Lostine River have long-since quieted. Over-the-shoulder views present Hurricane Divide, the Lostine River drainage, and distant snow-etched peaks. Dwarf and true huckleberry mat the floor.

Amid a soggy meadow at 3.5 miles, pass a sign for Maxwell Lake. False hellebore, pearly everlasting, and wild onion parade through the meadow. Pass between moist meadow and open forest where white-bark pine and subalpine fir weave a patchy cloak and rugged granite crests tower overhead.

With a sharp ascent of a wildflower-adorned bouldery meadow slope, top a rise for a captivating first impression of Maxwell Lake (4 miles): take in the azure lake, the outlet-threaded meadow, and the enfolding horseshoe ridge patched with snowfields.

A steep descent takes hikers to the lake's shore at 4.3 miles. A small central island punctuates the blue oval while the clear waters reveal a boulder-riddled bottom. The granite outcrops of shore limit campsites, preserving the tranquility. Mountain heather and grassy tufts spatter the rocky basin.

Hike southeast from the main lake to reach the second, smaller lake. Cross the outlet creek, mount a granite outcrop, and round toward the south ridge wall to find the charming, fish-filled lake beneath the rocky apron.

29 EAST FORK LOSTINE RIVER TRAIL

Round trip: 6.4 miles (to Lost Lake)
High point: 7,100 feet
Elevation change: 1,500 feet
Managed by: Eagle Cap Ranger District, Wallowa-Whitman National Forest
Maps: USFS Wallowa-Whitman National Forest, Imus Geographics Wallowa Mountains Eagle Cap Wilderness

This hike presents a glorious river drainage parting the high-mountain splendor of Eagle Cap Wilderness. The tour celebrates alpine forests and meadows, snowfield-etched ridges and peaks, side-canyon falls, and a sterling mountain stream—the East Fork Lostine River. Deer, elk, mountain goat, Clark's nutcracker, chickadee, nuthatch, and gray jay may share the canyon realm.

To reach this trail from OR 82 in Lostine, turn south at the sign for Lostine River Campgrounds on Lostine River Road/FR 8210, a paved and improved-surface road. In 17.5 miles the trail leaves the south end of Two Pan Campground.

Where the trail forks upon entering Eagle Cap Wilderness, go left

Lost Lake in early spring

for the East Fork Lostine River Trail (Trail 1662). Travel inland from the river ascending through a mixed forest of spruce, white fir, western larch, and lodgepole pine. Rocks, boulders, and outcrops litter the floor, interspersed by fairy slippers and yellow violets. Forest gaps extend westward looks at the granite and forested ridge dividing the Lostine river forks, with Hurricane Divide looming east.

The grade is moderate, and the trailbed is wide with a riddling of rocks and roots. The sound of the river proves a familiar companion, although river vistas are fleeting. At 1 mile, cross the East Fork Lostine River via a footbridge consisting of a single hewn log and a railing; youngsters may require supervision. The crystalline river spills over a bed of rounded colored rock; alders dress its banks.

As the trail switchbacks uphill after 1.6 miles, travel fir-spruce forest with aspen patches accenting the boulder slopes. Here clearings unveil fine views of Hurricane Divide, its sharp skyline, furrowed flank, spired evergreens, lingering snow, and glimmering side-creek falls. Later obtain a winning look out the Lostine River drainage. Scan for elk along the mid-reaches of Hurricane Divide. Deer may be spied nibbling lichen and moss from nearby rocks.

Where the trail tops out at 2.25 miles, travel the forest fringe edging a high meadow threaded by the slow, meandering East Fork Lostine River. Deep pools and golden gravel alter the appearance of the waterway. At 2.7 miles, a small falls graces the river.

Ahead lies a pond—a precursor to Lost Lake, which is actually a part of the East Fork where it broadens and slows to fill in the basin

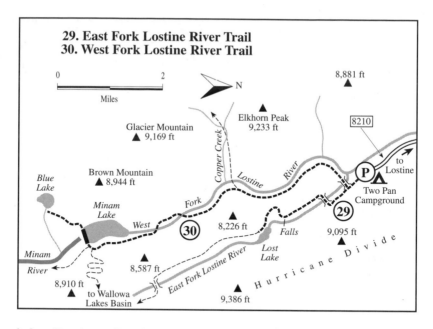

29. East Fork Lostine River Trail
30. West Fork Lostine River Trail

below Hurricane Divide and the west ridge. Small trees line its mirror waters.

Although not one of the signature lakes for the wilderness, elongated Lost Lake does make for a charming day-travel destination. Thru-trail hikers may proceed another 4 miles on the East Fork Lostine River Trail to access Mirror Lake and the neighboring blue lake waters of the acclaimed Wallowa Lakes Basin.

WEST FORK LOSTINE RIVER TRAIL

Round trip: 15 miles (to Blue Lake)
High point: 7,700 feet
Elevation change: 2,000 feet
Managed by: Eagle Cap Ranger District, Wallowa-Whitman National Forest
Maps: USFS Wallowa-Whitman National Forest, Imus Geographics Wallowa Mountains Eagle Cap Wilderness

This Eagle Cap Wilderness tour travels the majestic West Fork Lostine River drainage to visit Minam and Blue lakes. Nestled below Brown Mountain, Minam, the larger of the two natural lakes, is a long, oval platter with a small earthen dam at its south end. Blue Lake,

Blue Lake

round and mesmerizing, occupies the foot of a spiny white ridge for a more secluded retreat.

From OR 82 at Lostine, turn south at the sign for Lostine River Campgrounds onto Lostine River Road/FR 8210, a paved and graveled route. Go 17.5 miles to find the trailhead at the south end of Two Pan Campground.

Upon entering wilderness, bear right for the West Fork Lostine River/Minam Lake Trail (Trail 1670). The trail crosses the East Fork Lostine River, gathers early views of the West Fork (the main stem), and then climbs parallel to but removed from the river. Engelmann spruce, alder, white fir, western larch, and lodgepole pine shape a choked forest: myriad wildflowers contribute to the forest mat.

Pass granite outcrops, a bouldery slope with huckleberry, and a mature forest stand to again tour above the West Fork at 1.1 miles. A talus slope signals the 2.8-mile junction, where the Copper Creek Trail heads right. Keep left for Minam and Blue lakes.

Climb, skirting a meadow to travel a granite-boulder slope at the foot of the Lostine River divide. By 3.1 miles, discover open views of Copper Creek drainage, Elkhorn Peak, and the nearby granite domes.

The grade fluctuates as the trail passes in and out of an open lodgepole pine–subalpine fir complex. Amid a wildflower meadow at 4.1 miles, again draw closer to the West Fork Lostine River. Before long, a string of stones generally allows a dry crossing of the now creek-sized West Fork. Alternately tour meadow and subalpine fir forest before crossing back over the West Fork at 5.3 miles.

Soon, Brown Mountain comes into view: a reddish-brown volcanic crest suggests its name. At 5.8 miles, tag the shore of Minam Lake near the outlet. Mornings, the shallow glassy waters reflect the ridge of Brown Mountain and distant southern peaks.

The primary trail now rounds the east slope well above Minam Lake while angler paths travel closer to shore. With the forest-meadow floor being soft and moist, avoid off-trail excursions. Nearing the dam at 6.5 miles, come upon a three-way junction. A left leads to the popular Wallowa Lakes Basin; straight ahead the long-distance Minam River Trail (Trail 1673) begins. For Blue Lake Trail (Trail 1673A), travel atop the earthen dam and bear left upon exiting.

With a quick ascent, head southwest along a similar steep open-forested slope, bypassing a swath of trees tumbled by avalanche or wind storm. At 7.5 miles discover Blue Lake: deep, shimmering, and cobalt. White boulders, clustered subalpine fir, and weathered whitebark pines accent shore. A striking vertical white ridge with a razor-edged skyline and talus skirt watches over the basin. Green meadow drainages complement the glaring rock. Watch trout rise up through the clear waters, and harken the chiding of Clark's nutcrackers.

31 HURRICANE CREEK TRAIL

Round trip: 9 miles (to the first Hurricane Creek fording)
High point: 6,040 feet
Elevation change: 1,050 feet
Managed by: Eagle Cap Ranger District, Wallowa-Whitman National Forest
Maps: USFS Wallowa-Whitman National Forest, Imus Geographics Wallowa Mountains Eagle Cap Wilderness

Due to the steepness of its lower canyon and its middle meadow basins, Hurricane Creek presents perhaps the most continuous and spectacular views of any Eagle Cap drainage. Sacajawea Peak, Hurricane and Hurwal divides, the Matterhorn, and the exciting, changeable waters of Hurricane Creek urge hikers onward. A gorge-contained serial falls on Hurricane Creek and the continuous waterfall of Slick Rock Creek further win over visitors. As a gateway to the Wallowa Lakes Basin, this creek trail has all the requirements of a first-rate tour.

From the OR 3–OR 82 junction in Enterprise, drive east on OR 82 for 1.5 miles and turn right (south) at the sign for Hurricane Creek. In 4.9 miles proceed forward on a gravel road as Airport Lane arcs left to Joseph. At road's end in another 3.6 miles, reach the Hurricane Creek Trailhead, with parking, pit toilet, wilderness register, and hitching posts.

For Hurricane Creek Trail (Trail 1807), hike south through a forest-riparian corridor, pass the Falls Creek Trail turnoff, and cross gravelly Falls Creek via rocks or fording. At the crossing, enjoy upstream looks at Twin Peaks and downstream views of the Hurricane Creek confluence. Ahead an open grassy bench affords easy access to and unobstructed viewing of stair-stepping Hurricane Creek.

The trail then rolls uphill with a fairly steep grade, passing amid mixed conifers. At 0.4 mile, a spur

Sacajawea Peak

descends left to a rock promontory 20 feet above Hurricane Creek. The creek writes a wild signature with its steep-sided canyon, scoured bottom, and haphazard array of strewn logs and stumps. Upstream, glimpse majestic Sacajawea Peak (elevation 9,838 feet).

Where the trail passes through an avalanche zone of snapped trees, enter the wilderness (0.8 mile). Alternately tour forest and open meadow slopes with low-growing dogwoods. To the right tower the sheer rock and chiseled skyline of Hurricane Divide. To the left find the tree-mantled slopes of Hurwal Divide.

Where the canyon broadens, find a more tranquil Hurricane Creek threading through forest and scenic shrub flats. At 1.5 miles, cross Deadman Creek; in summer the water flows underground. Aspen and cottonwood decorate the drainage.

Upon re-entering the forest, enjoy easy strolling but temporarily lose views. From the aspen flat below Sacajawea Peak at 2.5 miles, look for

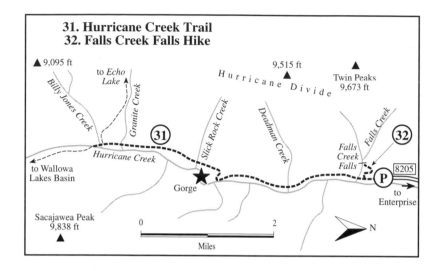

the trail to switchback uphill. A steep upstream gorge forces the trail higher up the slope.

In another 0.25 mile, look for a spur angling back to the left. Follow it a few strides to reach a safe falls viewing perch on the right. Here spy the serial falls on Hurricane Creek plummeting through the impressive steep-walled gorge. Admire both white chutes and the bubbling blue-green plunge pools. While the perch is generally safe, stay back from the edge and supervise children.

Next cross the long vertical spill of Slick Rock Creek, another stone crossing. Capture over-the-shoulder looks back at the gorge, and spy intriguing potholes along Hurricane Creek. Vertical fracturing and red dikes accentuate the cliff of Sacajawea Peak.

Return to forest. Where the trail next emerges in meadow (3.6 miles) find a 270-degree high peaks view. An unnamed creek threads the meadow. At 4.1 miles, cross Granite Creek, which drains Echo Lake. Early season hikers may need to wade.

At the next meadow break, glimpse the Matterhorn and find the cairn for the trail to Echo Lake, Trail 1824 (4.4 miles). With logs overlaying the start of this faint path to the right and an absence of maintenance in recent years, expect a challenging 3.6-mile trek to the lake. Allow adequate daylight for the journey.

Keep to Hurricane Creek Trail, which now follows meandering Billy Jones Creek to the point of its crossing; paired logs span its water. Traverse a meadow bank for close-up looks at Hurricane Creek and views of Sacajawea and Matterhorn.

At 4.5 miles the trail forks: a right leads to campsites; left leads to the Hurricane Creek fording. With quality views and creekside appreciation, the fording site offers a fine cap to the tour. Thru-trail hikers may continue upstream to reach Wallowa Lakes Basin in another 7.5 miles.

32 FALLS CREEK FALLS HIKE

Round trip: 1 mile (to falls)
High point: 5,300 feet
Elevation change: 300 feet
Managed by: Eagle Cap Ranger District, Wallowa-Whitman National
  Forest
Maps: USFS Wallowa-Whitman National Forest, Imus Geographics
  Wallowa Mountains Eagle Cap Wilderness

While short, this hike presents a complete wilderness snapshot, touring mid-elevation forest and meadow slope, ascending an avalanche-scoured creek drainage, visiting a picturesque waterfall, and extending looks at Eagle Cap Wilderness peaks. The hike begins on Hurricane Creek Trail (Hike 31), and may be continued beyond the falls, drawing ever skyward and growing more rugged. For the more adventurous, the trail halts at the Falls Creek headwater, Legore Lake (elevation 8,957 feet).

From the OR 3–OR 82 junction in Enterprise, drive east on OR 82 for 1.5 miles and turn right (south) at the sign for Hurricane Creek, traveling paved and gravel-surfaced road to reach Hurricane Creek Trailhead at road's end in 8.5 miles.

Head south on the marked Hurricane Creek Trail (Trail 1807), journeying upstream but removed from Hurricane Creek, a prized wilderness waterway. Spruce, fir, aspen, and small lodgepole pines make up the forest. Oregon grape and strawberry dot the grassy forest floor.

At 0.1 mile, bear right off the Hurricane Creek Trail, following narrow Falls Creek/Legore Trail (Trail 1807A); a tiny sign marks the turn. Make a mild ascent through a small meadow with gooseberry and currant that is removed from Falls Creek.

Where an avalanche tumbled and bent trees (0.3 mile), gain an open view of the 50-foot veiling falls coursing through a cleft, with snow-mantled Twin Peaks rising above the setting. The sight is especially dazzling at the threshold of hiking season (late April into early May), when the falls rages and more snow adorns the peak.

Descend into the rocky creek drainage following a gravel and rock path heading upstream just to the right of the main rocky streambed. A broad, clean-swept gray cliff rises to the right, while

Fairy slippers

Falls Creek Falls

a steep tree-and-cliff slope shapes the canyon's left wall. Over-the-shoulder looks find Chief Joseph Mountain.

With a steeper rocky ascent, reach the base of the falls at 0.5 mile. From the foot of the falls, admire the force and spray in spring. Later in the year, find a more tempered beauty, with tiered veils and skipping waters. Despite losing perspective on Twin Peaks, hikers still admire the steep flank, snowmelt ribbons, avalanche scars, and dark forest of Chief Joseph, looming to the east. Falls Creek holds raw beauty as it tumbles away from the falls.

For hikers unable to negotiate the rocks, the falls view at 0.3 mile amply satisfies. For hikers continuing beyond the falls, be aware that the trail is no longer on the official roster and is no longer maintained.

33 CHIEF JOSEPH TRAIL

Round trip: 4.4 miles (to Wallowa Lake vista)
High point: 5,000 feet
Elevation change: 600 feet
Managed by: Eagle Cap Ranger District, Wallowa-Whitman National
Forest
Maps: USFS Wallowa-Whitman National Forest, Imus Geographics
Wallowa Mountains Eagle Cap Wilderness

This trail travels the flank of Chief Joseph Mountain (elevation 9,617 feet), named for the famous Nez Perce chief. It was Chief Joseph, Young Joseph, who led a desperate flight for freedom across Hells Canyon, through Idaho, and into Montana before surrendering to the U.S. Army in 1877. The grave of Old Chief Joseph, his father, now occupies the north end of Wallowa Lake.

On this hike, visit sparkling waterways and an exciting BC Creek falls. Vistas include the jewel-like waters of Wallowa Lake, its classic glacial moraine, and the surrounding Wallowa high peaks.

To reach Chief Joseph Trail from Joseph, take OR 82 south for 6 miles, bear left at the fork, and follow Upper Power House Road to its end in 1 mile. The trailhead is opposite the South Unit of Wallowa Lake State Park. Follow the signs for West Fork Wallowa River Trail (Trail 1820).

At the 0.25-mile junction on the West Fork Wallowa River Trail, the 7-mile Chief Joseph Trail (Trail 1803) branches right to scale the east flank of Chief Joseph Mountain halting at a vista point shy of the summit. Go right, traveling upstream along the east bank of the West Fork to pass 100 feet above the rock-bound river gorge. Ponderosa pine, white fir, and Rocky Mountain maple frame the path. Wild strawberry grows in the rock outcroppings.

Next cross the West Fork footbridge and quickly leave behind the river. With a switchbacking ascent, draw inland to the base of the ridge. Now ascend through a forest of lodgepole pine, larch, aspen, and mountain mahogany. Penetrating light supports a rich grass floor. By 0.75 mile, hike below a rocky slope where pikas whistle from unseen nooks. Amid the rocks find showings of Oregon grape, bracken fern, and thimbleberry. Wallowa Lake views now contribute to the tour.

At 0.9 mile, cross the footbridge over BC Creek, a beautiful white-bubbling waterway punctuated by serial falls and cascades coursing over rock terraces. Amid a tiny flat, find views of another falls, Wallowa Lake, and looming southeast, the 8,200-foot Mount Howard, which is named for the U.S. Army general in charge during the Nez Perce uprising and flight.

The trail grows rockier upon entering Eagle Cap Wilderness (1.1 miles). Gather more lake views and spy the tramway streaking up Mount Howard. As the trail continues to climb, a thicker forest denies lake views.

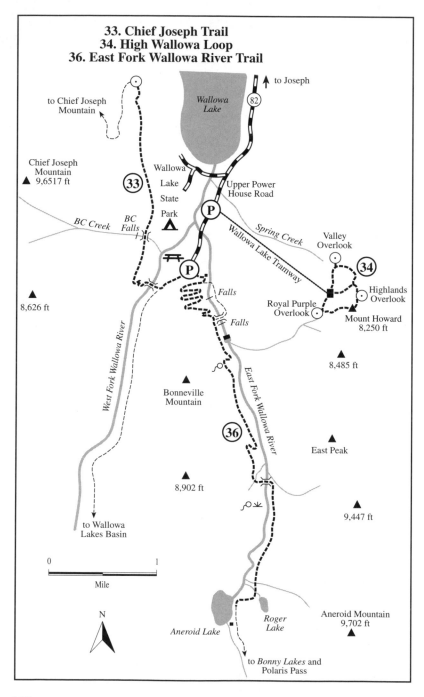

33. Chief Joseph Trail
34. High Wallowa Loop
36. East Fork Wallowa River Trail

Wallowa River hiker bridge

At 2 miles, ten spectacular ponderosa pines cluster trailside, marking the start of a series of vista clearings that continue over the next 0.2 mile. From the turnaround vantage at 2.2 miles, overlook the glacial moraine of Wallowa Lake, Mount Howard, and the patchwork fields stretching north. Thistle, pearly everlasting, balsamroot, and Indian paintbrush color the openings.

Hikers have the option of continuing the tour, steadily drawing skyward to the closing vista at 7 miles. Locate the next set of switchbacks at 2.75 miles, as the more serious ascent begins.

34 HIGH WALLOWA LOOP

Loop trip: 2 miles
High point: 8,250 feet
Elevation change: 100 feet
Managed by: Wallowa Lake Tramway
Map: Wallowa Lake Tramway brochure

By lightening the billfold and boarding a gondola, hikers step out onto the region's most easily accessed summit trail system. Atop Mount Howard find a series of simple interlocking loops that visit three summit promontories for an exciting Hells Canyon–Wallowa country overview. Admire the leading 9,000-footers of the Wallowa Mountain Range and Idaho's Seven Devils in the distance. On clear days identify features of four states: Oregon, Idaho, Washington, and Montana. Often stiff, chill winds wash over the summit, invigorating flesh and spirit.

From Joseph, take OR 82 south for 6 miles and bear left on Upper Power House Road to find the entrance for Wallowa Lake Tramway on

Mount Howard summit

the left. Purchase a ticket to travel the steepest vertical-lift gondola in North America to the top of Mount Howard. The tramway operates daily late May through September, 10:00 A.M. to 4:00 P.M. Foul weather may affect operating schedules, so phone before visiting.

During the 15-minute tram ride, the four-passenger gondolas travel 19,300 feet of cable to the summit terminal (elevation 8,250 feet). The ride itself offers a superb view of Wallowa Lake, the Joseph Valley, Chief Joseph Mountain, BC Creek basin, Hurwal Divide, and Mount Howard.

From the summit terminal, hike the 2-mile outer circuit. A counter-clockwise tour travels first to Royal Purple Overlook, on to the Summit Overlook atop Mount Howard's high point, and back via the Valley Overlook; the trail's layout is in the tramway brochure. While en route enjoy a fourth vista, Highlands Overlook.

This well-marked interpretive trail (Trail 1813) travels a stirring high-country landscape of alpine meadows, fringe forests of wind-shaped whitebark pines and skirted subalpine firs, and lichen-encrusted rock outcrops. Lupine, western yarrow, heather, aster, bunchgrass, and dwarf huckleberry vegetate the meadows. Chipmunks and chickadees divert the eye.

On the vista round-up, Royal Purple Overlook (0.2 mile) presents the Wallowa high peaks, Royal Purple Canyon, and the east and west forks of the Wallowa River drainage. At 0.5 mile, Summit Overlook extends looks toward Hells Canyon, Seven Devils, and Freezeout Saddle. Here too, view East Peak and the trail that travels it. Shortly after, reach Highlands Overlook and scan the landscape of silvered snags from the 1989 McCully Creek Fire.

Complete the vista round-up at Valley Overlook with views of Wallowa Lake, the imposing Wallowa front range, the stunning Imnaha River drainage, and the valley patchwork. Juniper dots the metamorphic rock of the vantage point. A 0.5-mile hike returns travelers to the summit terminal.

35 WEST FORK WALLOWA RIVER TRAIL–LAKES BASIN LOOP

Round trip: 30 miles
High point: 8,450 feet
Elevation change: 3,900 feet
Managed by: Eagle Cap Ranger District, Wallowa-Whitman National Forest
Maps: USFS Wallowa-Whitman National Forest, Imus Geographics Wallowa Mountains Eagle Cap Wilderness

This choice but demanding hike is a tribute to the regal domain of Eagle Cap Wilderness. On the 30-mile quest, journey along the chiseled drainage of a crystalline river, tour a superb high-country meadow, string past six inviting cobalt lakes, and cross a challenging skyline pass. Throughout the hike, spectacular views engulf the traveler. Discover granite domes, imposing divides, and glacial bowls and valleys. Snowmelt waterfalls and an icy river crossing punctuate travel.

To reach the trailhead from Joseph, go south on OR 82 for 6 miles, bearing left on Upper Power House Road. In another mile reach the trailhead at road's end opposite South Unit, Wallowa Lake State Park.

Follow signs for the West Fork Wallowa River Trail (Trail 1820), bearing right near the start of the hike; the east fork trail heads left. At the 0.25-mile junction proceed forward, pursuing the West Fork upstream into Eagle Cap Wilderness. In summer, a choking dust may blanket the early miles of this popular hiker-horse trail.

Travel a semi-open mixed conifer forest, interrupted by talus slopes. Hurwal Divide looms to the west; study its flank for moving snowfields, which are actually mountain goats. Secondary trails branch to the river.

Continue along the river, bypassing Ice Lake Trail (Trail 1808) at 2.8 miles. Although above the West Fork, enjoy filtered river views, with the river's rush a constant. Upstream from the Adam Creek confluence, the size of the river is dramatically reduced. Western views feature Craig Mountain and isolated campsites call to backpackers who got a late-day start.

Side creeks mark off distance as the trail passes between meadow and forest. Lily, aster, yarrow, paintbrush, and columbine splash color throughout the greenery.

In the shadow of an impressive cliff at 6 miles, find elongated Six Mile Meadow and the Lakes Basin Loop junction. Coyotes sometimes prowl the meadow. Other times, deer or elk may call hikers to an admiring halt. Campsites are located along the forest fringe.

For a clockwise lakes basin tour, continue upstream along the West Fork Wallowa River toward Hawkins Pass. At 7.75 mile, light-colored peaks dress the head of the canyon and the climb accelerates. Well

113

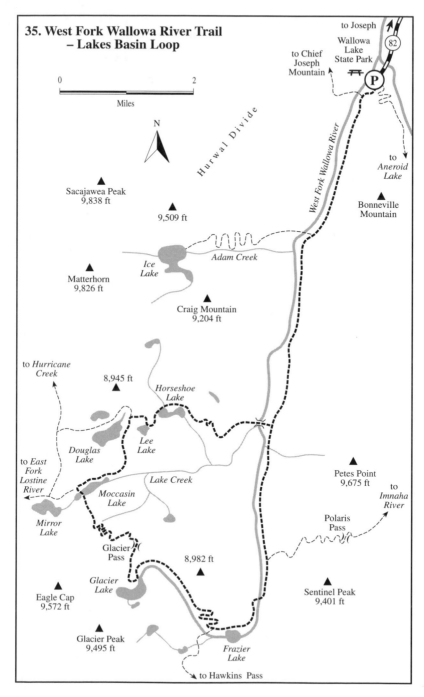

35. West Fork Wallowa River Trail – Lakes Basin Loop

to Joseph

Wallowa Lake State Park

82

to Chief Joseph Mountain

P

0 — 2

Miles

N

Hurwal Divide

to Aneroid Lake

West Fork Wallowa River

Sacajawea Peak
9,838 ft

▲ 9,509 ft

Bonneville Mountain

Adam Creek

Ice Lake

▲ Matterhorn
9,826 ft

▲ Craig Mountain
9,204 ft

to Hurricane Creek

8,945 ft ▲

Horseshoe Lake

Lee Lake

Douglas Lake

to East Fork Lostine River

Lake Creek

Moccasin Lake

▲ Petes Point
9,675 ft

to Imnaha River

Mirror Lake

Polaris Pass

Glacier Pass

▲ 8,982 ft

Glacier Lake

▲ Eagle Cap
9,572 ft

▲ Sentinel Peak
9,401 ft

▲ Glacier Peak
9,495 ft

Frazier Lake

to Hawkins Pass

Glacier Peak and Lake

above the river, bypass the Polaris Trail (Trail 1831) and skirt a cliff overlooking a West Fork gorge. With the crossing of a high meadow below the east canyon wall, reach a chilly West Fork fording (9.75 miles); watch footing.

With a switchback into forest, journey toward the canyon head reaching Frazier Lake, a shallow green pool framed by a bold ridge at 10.5 miles. Tinsel chutes and glaring snowfields accent the ridge while a smaller lake rests at its foot.

At the upcoming junction head right for Glacier Pass on Trail 1806, traversing granite-boulder slopes with alcoves of fir. Avoid the trail to Hawkins Pass. After 12.5 miles, Eagle Cap becomes a familiar friend.

Reach Glacier Lake at 13 miles. Nestled below Eagle Cap and Glacier Peak and fed by Benson Glacier, Glacier Lake shines clear, deep, and blue—the epitome of high-country splendor. Small islands pierce the lake's surface while alpine wildflowers spangle its shore.

Drawing above Glacier Lake, spy a smaller, upper lake, and within a mile top Glacier Pass (elevation 8,450 feet) for a stirring measure of one's accomplishment. A sharp descent on an exposed slope follows. Peer out the East Fork Lostine River and Hurricane Creek drainages to admire Hurricane Divide, the Matterhorn, and Moccasin and Mirror lakes.

Cross a drainage at 14.75 miles to enter a series of switchbacks, still descending steeply. With the next drainage crossing, travel meadows of wildflowers and wild onion to top a rise at 16 miles. Where the trail again dips, find Moccasin Lake. Quick drop-offs and hypnotic blue waters characterize the lakes of Wallowa Lakes Basin.

An isthmus and stepping stones allow hikers to cross at the neck of this parted lake body. Upon reaching the opposite shore, keep to the loop as it arcs right, rounding the northwest slope of Moccasin Lake to return to the West Fork Wallowa River. The trail to the left leads to the East Fork Lostine River. Across the lake, spy Eagle Cap's fractured face.

The partially forested route then undulates between lake basins. Bear right at all junctions to visit Douglas Lake (18 miles), Lee Lake (19 miles), and Horseshoe Lake (20 miles). Stroll the length of Horseshoe Lake before entering a series of steady downhill switchbacks on Trail 1810, returning to fuller forest.

At 23.5 miles, follow Lake Creek downstream through a stand of dead spruce. At the West Fork confluence, cross footbridges over Lake Creek and the West Fork. At the north end of Six Mile Meadow, close the loop at 24 miles. Now head left from the junction to return to the trailhead (30 miles).

36 EAST FORK WALLOWA RIVER TRAIL

Round trip: 12 miles (to Aneroid Lake)
High point: 7,600 feet
Elevation change: 2,950 feet
Managed by: Eagle Cap Ranger District, Wallowa-Whitman National Forest
Maps: USFS Wallowa-Whitman National Forest, Imus Geographics Wallowa Mountains Eagle Cap Wilderness

While climbing nearly 3,000 vertical feet, this well-paced trail provides a comfortable introduction to the high-country splendor enfolding Aneroid Lake (see map p. 110). The East Fork Wallowa River proves an engaging host with the excitement of its plummeting lower waters and tranquil meandering headwater. Early views feature Wallowa Lake and Chief Joseph. Upstream, East Peak, Aneroid Mountain, and Petes Point watch over the proceedings.

Take OR 82 south from Joseph for 6 miles and bear left on Upper Power House Road. In another mile, reach the trailhead at road's end opposite the South Unit, Wallowa Lake State Park.

Following the signs for East Fork Wallowa River Trail (Trail 1804), hike southeast past the kiosk on a wide dirt lane, bearing left up the hill for Aneroid Lake. Near an old weathered building at 0.1 mile, look for the road/trail to turn sharply right, continuing a moderate ascent through open fir–lodgepole pine forest. At the fork at 0.2 mile, the foot-horse trail proceeds forward, as the "cat road" to the powerhouse dam swings left; keep to the foot-horse trail.

Along with occasional larch or ponderosa pine, ninebark, ocean spray, aspen, and Rocky Mountain maple intersperse the forest. With the onset of switchbacks, catch glimpses of the shimmery Wallowa Lake platter. Chief Joseph Mountain appears through a notch in the

Aneroid Lake

western ridge; Mount Howard rises to the east. At a switchback at 0.6 mile, overlook a thundering 20-foot vertical falls on the river. A short side spur delivers a better angle.

By 1 mile enter the river canyon proper, touring a talus-shrub slope noisy with alarmed pikas. At this point, the path narrows to trail-width. Unobstructed lake views enthrall travelers, adding the valley tapestry, distant Blue Mountains, and dancing veils of morning fog. Round and ascend the west canyon wall, traveling amid fuller forest.

Overlook the tumbling white ribbon of the East Fork where the trail switchbacks uphill to a bridge linking the cat road and trail at 1.75 mile. A detour onto the bridge presents a square-on look at another racing river falls twisting through rock. Keep to the west canyon wall, never crossing the bridge, to continue the tour to Aneroid Lake.

At 2 miles bypass the small dam, with its metal-grate spillway, penstock, and holding pond. Upstream the river drops less steeply. At 2.25 miles enter Eagle Cap Wilderness, drawing ever deeper into the canyon. A few springs dampen the trail and give rise to false hellebore bogs.

Alternately tour open-cathedral forest and meadow slopes. Cross-canyon views find East Peak, with Aneroid Mountain farther up the canyon. Gradually the meadows show an alpine mix of grasses and wildflowers, and deer sometimes cross paths with hikers.

At 3.75 miles, cross a side drainage via rocks or logs, and in another 0.1 mile cross a footbridge over the East Fork Wallowa River. Upon crossing, look for the main trail to arc left through lodgepole pine forest; a secondary trail travels upstream. Stay on the main trail.

At 4.25 miles find a split-traffic flow. Bear right on the lower trail when heading up-canyon; outbound traffic travels the upper one. The newfound narrowness of the trail and a plunging slope necessitate this separation. Contouring the slope, overlook the river and gaze out the East Fork Canyon to the valley.

Next, travel the broad forest-and-meadow basin where past beaver activity has left behind shallow ponds, some now breached. Cross a side stream via a trio of logs and resume the ascent, avoiding closed sections of old trail. At 5.25 miles, a spur to the right enters a meadow for an open-aisle view to Petes Point (elevation 9,675 feet).

Cross a meandering meadow stream via rustic footbridges and culverts to reach Roger Lake (5.5 miles). Spurs venture left to this shallow bat-winged lake at the foot of Aneroid Mountain. Touring its treed point and soggy meadow shore, round up skyline views, including East Peak.

The East Fork trail skirts above the west shore of Roger Lake, ascending and weaving to Aneroid Lake (6 miles). Upon arrival at the lake, signs point the way to campsites. Private cabins occupy the south shore; no trespassing.

Like a large turquoise teardrop, Aneroid Lake shines up from its steep-sided bowl at the foot of Petes Point. Steep rock and scree slopes plunge to the water while a serene, rich meadow graces the south shore. Still waters reflect the imposing rock realm and spired trees of the shore. The river, breached beaver ponds, and sparkling Aneroid Lake, all support trout.

37 McCULLY CREEK TRAIL

Round trip: 11.2 miles (to upper McCully Basin)
High point: 7,900 feet
Elevation change: 2,300 feet
Managed by: Eagle Cap Ranger District, Wallowa-Whitman National Forest
Maps: USFS Wallowa-Whitman National Forest, Imus Geographics Wallowa Mountains Eagle Cap Wilderness

This seldom-traveled trail (Trail 1812) follows McCully Creek upstream to a serene meadow basin below Aneroid Mountain and East Peak. Although McCully Creek accompanies the tour, the creek remains for the most part a mystery until the later miles. Begin amid the regenerating Canal Burn habitat, legacy of a 1989 fire.

To reach McCully Creek Trail from Joseph, turn east off OR 82 on East Wallowa Avenue, following the signs for Ferguson Ridge. Go 5.2 miles and turn right on Tucker Down Road, a wide improved-surface road. In 2.9 miles bear right upon crossing a cattle guard, and in another 1.7 miles cross McCully Creek, now on FR 3920. The marked trailhead is 200 feet past the creek on the right.

Start next to the stock-loading ramp, touring a ghost forest interspersed by live trees. In 50 feet a cairn marks the site for the horse fording of McCully Creek. Hike 50 feet farther upstream to cross via a three-log bridge, absent a railing and with post-fire gaps; exercise care in crossing.

The trail then weaves up the opposite slope to reach a rough, lightly used secondary forest road, FR 012 (0.1 mile). Follow it left, admiring an unnamed 9,000-foot peak ahead. Over-the-shoulder looks find Hells Canyon and Idaho's Seven Devils.

Pass into live forest, and where the road forks at 0.6 mile, bear left for the trail. The jeep trail to the right leads to Mount Howard. At 0.9 mile reach the end of the drivable forest road, coming to a wilderness self-registration box, campsite, and hitching post. The foot-horse trail ahead remains wide for a spell.

The rolling trail keeps within sound of McCully Creek, seldom traveling more than 100 vertical feet from the waterway. Save for a brief return to the Canal Burn at 1.3 miles, an open-cathedral forest houses the trail.

McCully Basin

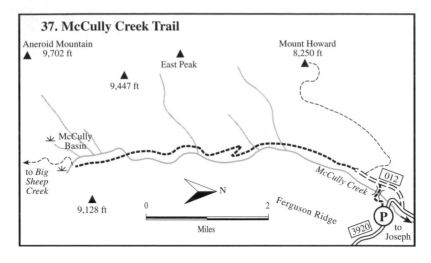

37. McCully Creek Trail

At 2.5 miles, enter Eagle Cap Wilderness. Ahead the trail switch-backs to travel a higher contour along the western slope of McCully Creek Canyon. At 3.5 miles, capture the first genuine look at McCully Creek since the footbridge. The clear stream courses over rock and boulder, with icicle adornments in the fall.

The grade allows hikers to comfortably accomplish the elevation gain. An occasional spring may muddy the trail. With another creek view at 4.1 miles, again switchback to travel a higher line above McCully Creek. Before long the canyon broadens.

Where the trail forks at 4.7 miles, proceed forward for the McCully Creek crossing (4.75 miles), accomplished via stones or fording. The path to the right leads uphill to left-over structures from an abandoned mining claim. From the crossing, the trail drifts away from the creek to tour the meadow-forest mosaic of McCully Basin.

At 5 miles, skirt a broad wildflower meadow with pockets of low shrubs and a grand panorama. Here, Aneroid Mountain, the East Peak Ridge, sawtooth crags, a coffin-like feature, and long, smooth saddles shape an impressive skyline amphitheater—a setting sure to suggest the unstrapping of the pack.

As hikers proceed up-canyon, a few cairns help identify the faint meadow-forest trail. Tiny headwater streams slice the way. At 5.2 miles, climb to the upper basin (5.6 miles).

Gentian and heather dot the upper basin. Here the trail to the mountain pass virtually disappears, signaling the turnaround for day hikers. Thru-trail hikers will have to scout for trail fragments and other clues to reach the pass.

OREGON WALLOWAS, EAGLE CAP WILDERNESS SOUTH

East Fork Falls

38 HORSE RANCH TRAIL

Round trip 15.6 miles (to Minam River)
High point: 5,842 feet (trailhead)
Elevation change: 2,250 feet
Managed by: Eagle Cap Ranger District, Wallowa-Whitman National Forest
Maps: USFS Wallowa-Whitman National Forest, Imus Geographics Wallowa Mountains Eagle Cap Wilderness

Horse Ranch Trail (Trail 1908) descends from a Wallowa Mountain plateau to the pristine Minam River, passing through historic Red's Horse Ranch, which is now owned by the U.S. Forest Service. Popularity threatens this resource, so admire as you pass, then disperse from the area. A caretaker resides at the ranch.

The terrain along this hike resembles Hells Canyon as much as the Wallowa high country: as you travel, view basalt-tiered grassland rims, rocky ridges and summits, and an occasional dusting of snow on the high country.

En route, enjoy an interlude with the Little Minam River. At the close of the trail, the dazzling Minam Wild and Scenic River casts its spell.

From OR 237 in Cove, turn east on French Street (opposite the high school) for Moss Springs Campground. French Street then bends into Mill Creek Lane, which later becomes FR 6220. Follow these paved

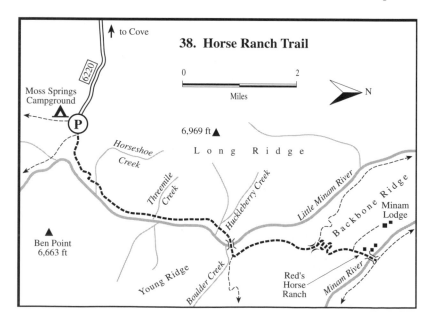

Minam River

and gravel routes for 8.4 miles, reaching the campground. There go right to find the trailhead in 0.2 mile.

Round the trailhead sign, descending east into the wilderness on a dusty foot-horse trail; do not take the Lodgepole Trail, which heads right on former FR 6220.410. Mountain hemlock, lodgepole pine, larch, and fir weave an open forest, with dwarf huckleberry and prince's pine growing below. During fall hunting season, the trail receives especially heavy use.

Upon entering Eagle Cap Wilderness, bear left at the trail fork, proceeding toward the Minam River. By 0.5 mile, the moderate-grade trail wraps across a steep meadow slope, extending early canyon views. Pass between meadow and forest stand, contouring the steep western slope above the glint and rush of the Little Minam River.

At 1.5 miles ford Horseshoe Creek. Alders frame the drainage; downfalls litter the immediate woods. By 2 miles, replace overlooks of the Little Minam River with bankside seating.

The rolling trail still pursues the Little Minam River downstream, often separated by a steep wooded slope. Bride's bonnet, arnica, and dogwood lend floral accents. At 3.1 miles cross the reliable side tributary of Threemile Creek, as the forest mix becomes mostly fir-spruce. Yews, an uncommon find in the eastern Oregon forest, also border the trail.

After crossing Huckleberry Creek via stones or wading, cross the horse bridge spanning the Little Minam River near the Boulder Creek confluence (4.5 miles). Past the bridge, look for the trail (Trail 1908) to arc left toward the Minam River; signs mark the junction.

Now contour the eastern forested slope farther removed from the Little Minam. Large-diameter trees and a handful of mossy boulders enrich the tour. After 6 miles, drier ridges of ponderosa pine and mountain mahogany house the trail. At the 6.5-mile junction, bear right and traverse narrow Backbone Ridge for a first impression of the Minam River drainage, the meadow flat of Red's Horse Ranch, and arid Sheep and Washboard ridges across the way.

Briefly trace the ridge spine before zigzagging downhill to the river and ranch. At 7.2 miles spy a developed spring below to the right. At 7.5 miles reach a rustic pole gateway to Red's Horse Ranch; to the left lies the privately owned Minam Lodge.

Enter the ranch, crossing a grassy airstrip. From the nearby woods, pileated woodpeckers deliver a raucous greeting. Trail signs point hikers around a corral, still active with horses, and past a weathered barn to yet another gate. Pass through this gate, traveling a small fenced pasture. To the left lie the log ranch house and now-closed riverside cabins; elk horns dress the site.

Exit the north end of the pasture and hike up and over a rise to reach a horse bridge over the Minam River. On the opposite shore, the Minam River Trail (Trail 1673) parallels the river in both directions. Suitable campsites dot the ponderosa pine flat of the east shore, but avoid these sites and instead look for ones farther away from the ranch.

The Minam enchants with its clear flow and scenic bends. Return as you came or explore the river corridor. Only the occasional small plane landing downstream at rustic Minam Lodge breaks the wilderness silence.

39 NORTH FORK CATHERINE CREEK TRAIL

Round trip: 10 miles (to Catherine Creek Meadows)
High point: 5,650 feet
Elevation change: 1,450 feet
Managed by: Eagle Cap Ranger District, Wallowa-Whitman National Forest
Maps: USFS Wallowa-Whitman National Forest, Imus Geographics Wallowa Mountains Eagle Cap Wilderness

This tranquil wilderness tour (Trail 1905) explores the forest, meadow, and riparian habitats of the North Fork Catherine Creek drainage to end at either a sealed cabin or a scenic meadow shore. Framed by rounded wooded ridges and traveled by sparkling tributaries, the expansive grassy plain of privately held Catherine Creek Meadows suggests a leisurely stroll; keep to the trail. Grouse, deer, bear, or bugling elk may enrich a tour.

To reach North Fork Catherine Creek Trail from Union, go 11 miles southeast on OR 203 and turn east onto Catherine Creek Lane/FR 7785, a gravel route. Stay on FR 7785 to North Fork Catherine Creek Campground and the trailhead at 5.7 miles.

From the upper end of the campground, follow North Fork Catherine Creek for a rolling upstream tour. Travel the west shore, climbing a mostly open slope with dispersed ponderosa pine and basalt outcrops. Trailside vegetation includes currant, lupine, larkspur, strawberry, and bracken fern. For much of the journey, pass within sound but not sight of the creek. Side streams may require seasonal wading.

Gradually fir and spruce fill in the forest, but enough light penetrates for a flourishing meadow understory. At 1.25 miles, cross the horse bridge over the North Fork Catherine Creek. The glistening black creek flows 12 feet wide over a rocky streambed; riffles and cascades vary its look. Dogwood, snowberry, alder, and Rocky Mountain maple crowd the banks. Ahead waits a brief, more steeply climbing trail segment.

Next tour the eastern shore, where in autumn, trailside huckleberry patches may sidetrack hikers. Cottonwoods rise above the creek while cross-canyon views present a steep open-sloped ridge with a treed summit. At 1.8 miles, pass through a black boulder field to cross the larger side stream of Chop Creek. Upon entering Eagle Cap Wilderness, cross Jim Creek below a picturesque 3-foot cascade.

Just past Jim Creek, spurs descend left to a thin meadow abutting the clear-rippling North Fork Catherine Creek. The main trail contours the slope overlooking the meadow, small springs may muddy the way.

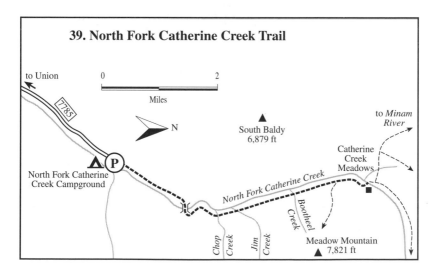

39. North Fork Catherine Creek Trail

to Union

7785

0   2

Miles

N

to *Minam River*

South Baldy
6,879 ft

Catherine
Creek
Meadows

North Fork Catherine
Creek Campground

P

North Fork Catherine Creek

Bootheel Creek

Chop Creek

Jim Creek

Meadow Mountain
7,821 ft

North Fork Catherine Creek

At 3.1 miles cross Bootheel Creek for a mostly wooded tour, with the rushing North Fork sounding in the background. The trail advances via rolling ascents with easy to moderate grades. Look for the forest mix to vary; black lichens drape the larch.

Where the canyon yawns at 4.3 miles, pass through an old gate to travel the forest fringe of broad, expansive Catherine Creek Meadows. The enfolding wooded ridges present a gentler aspect than the granite cliffs encountered elsewhere in the Wallowas. Cross a tiny stream to travel the upper edge of the meadow for a better appreciation of the grassland's size and texture.

Hike past a bare trail post at 4.6 miles, and soon after, traverse the main meadow to an upper spring-fed meadow and trail fork (4.9 miles). Go left to end along the bank of the North Fork Catherine Creek; hike right to conclude at a small rustic cabin amid a spruce grove. Washtubs, buckets, and grills dress the walls of the boarded-up cabin; do not disturb the site. From the alternative creek ending 300 feet from the trail fork, backpackers may choose to continue on the North Fork Catherine Creek Trail: ford and hike up canyon to the Minam River, another 9 miles distant.

40 WEST EAGLE CREEK TRAIL

Round trip: 12.8 miles (to Traverse Lake)
High point: 7,850 feet
Elevation change: 2,400 feet
Managed by: Eagle Cap Ranger District, Wallowa-Whitman National Forest
Maps: USFS Wallowa-Whitman National Forest, Imus Geographics Wallowa Mountains Eagle Cap Wilderness

This Eagle Cap Wilderness hike joins a wonderful canyon tour with visits to two mountain lakes—Echo and Traverse. West Eagle Creek Trail (Trail 1934) begins in picturesque West Eagle Meadows and strings through high-country splendor. Travel spruce-fir forest, wade sparkling, cold West Eagle Creek, cross granite outcrops, spy a hanging waterfall, and revel in canyon vistas.

From OR 203, 6 miles north of Medical Springs, 14 miles south of Union, turn east on FR 77/Eagle Creek Road, a gravel road that becomes unsuitable for passenger vehicles after 9.6 miles. Go 5 miles past the "rough road" sign, and turn left for West Eagle Trailhead to find parking and a register in 0.4 mile.

Hike north (upstream), touring the eastern edge of West Eagle Meadows where cattle may graze. Morning veils of fog drift across the lush grass-and-lupine expanse. Pockets of hellebore, low shrubs, and lone trees complete the mosaic.

Travel a conifer forest, hiking past a trail cairn for the western terminus of Fake Creek Trail at 0.2 mile (Trail 1914). Next cross Fake

Traverse Lake

Creek via log or wading and traverse meadow, before resuming a rolling tour at the foot of the forested slope.

At 0.8 mile ford West Eagle Creek. Early-season hikers may find water topping the knee and a much wider stream, without the gravel bars of late summer. Willow and alder grow along the creek. Enter the wilderness, meandering amid larger trees, crossing meadow slopes, and stepping over ribbony side waters. At 1.2 miles catch glimpses of the enfolding canyon.

With a zigzag crossing over granite outcrop, admire a cascade on West Eagle Creek, and at 1.9 miles reach the second crossing. In late summer, cross the creek via gravel bars, rock-hopping, or a generous log. A succession of switchbacks now mounts the west canyon wall.

At 2.3 miles view a hanging waterfall on the East Fork West Eagle Creek. In spring it thunders; in fall admire a series of shimmery braids. Travel a rock-and-shrub mantled slope interrupted by fingers of forest. At 2.5 miles reach Tombstone Lake Junction and proceed forward for Trail Creek.

Nameless, trailless peaks overlook the trail, as it switchbacks between the West Eagle and East Fork West Eagle creek drainages. The tour grows more exposed with the well-paced switchbacks coming as regular as breaths. By 2.9 miles, travel above West Eagle alone. Amid the granite talus, watch for pikas—tiny, big-eared rodents with high-pitched squeaks.

At 4.25 miles, cross West Eagle Creek, and ascend a log corduroy through wet meadow, passing amid elbow-high vegetation. A sun-spangled pond at the foot of a craggy ridge is a harbinger of the bigger lakes to come.

Switchbacks resume. Pass a couple of campsites before reaching the trail fork at Echo Lake (4.8 miles). A 150-foot spur to the right leads to the shore of Echo Lake, which is pretty despite a small irrigation dam. A ragged ridge stands watch, its slopes plunging to the glistening bowl.

On the main trail, skirt above the north shore of Echo Lake; spurs wiggle to the water. At 5.3 miles, cross the inlet spring and soon after climb for Traverse Lake. Tour slopes of granite, dwarf huckleberry, and bunchgrass, with wild onion in the alpine meadows. Deer may startle upon approach. At 6.1 miles come upon an exciting Echo Lake–West Eagle Canyon overlook.

At 6.4 miles, reach the palette-shaped water of Traverse Lake snuggled below a conical rock peak. A sandy beach-ring betrays that this lake, too, supplies irrigation water. End travel here, or proceed along the north shore to Wonker Pass, Trail Creek, and points beyond.

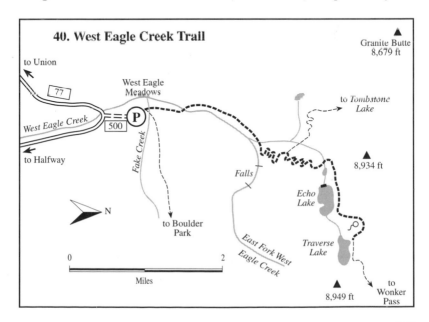

40. West Eagle Creek Trail

to Union

West Eagle Meadows

77

West Eagle Creek

500

P

Fake Creek

to Halfway

N

to Boulder Park

Falls

East Fork West Eagle Creek

0   2

Miles

Granite Butte 8,679 ft

to Tombstone Lake

8,934 ft

Echo Lake

Traverse Lake

8,949 ft

to Wonker Pass

High Wallowas, Fake Creek Trail

41   FAKE CREEK TRAIL

Round trip: 6 miles (to ridge saddle)
High point: 7,400 feet
Elevation change: 2,500 feet
Managed by: Eagle Cap Ranger District, Wallowa-Whitman National Forest
Maps: USFS Wallowa-Whitman National Forest, Imus Geographics Wallowa Mountains Eagle Cap Wilderness

This day hike begins at the eastern terminus of the 6-mile-long Fake Creek Trail (Trail 1914) and climbs west to a ridge saddle above Boulder Park, the midway point. This stamina-testing climb delivers rewarding vistas, both approaching and atop the saddle. Lightly traveled, the trail affords solitude, opportunities for wildlife encounters, and a strong appreciation for the Wallowa wilds. Thru-trail hikers may follow the full length of the trail, accessing West Eagle Creek Trail (Hike 40) and Echo, Traverse, or Tombstone lakes.

From OR 203 in Medical Springs, turn southeast on Eagle Creek Drive for Boulder Park. The road surface quickly changes to gravel. In 1.6 miles, turn left onto FR 67/Big Creek Road. In another 13.5 miles, go left (north) on FR 77 for 0.7 mile. There turn right on FR 7755, go 3.2 miles, and turn left onto FR 7755.090. In 100 feet find trailhead parking and a picnic area to the right. The trail follows narrow, rough FR 7755.090 uphill to the wilderness.

Ascend the narrow rock-studded road, veering left at the cabins. The

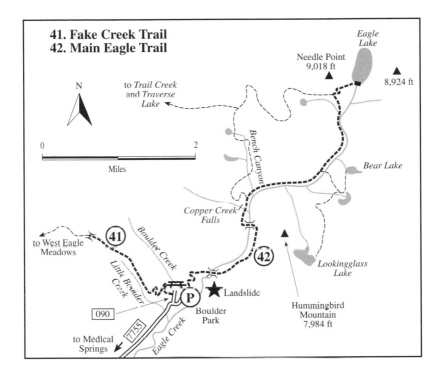

41. Fake Creek Trail
42. Main Eagle Trail

roadbed further deteriorates before entering Eagle Cap Wilderness as a hiker trail at 0.2 mile. Traverse the slope, passing between a semi-open mixed forest of fir, ponderosa pine, and western larch and open meadow slopes. From the meadow breaks, overlook the landslide above Boulder Park that altered the flow of Eagle Creek. In places, grasses overwhelm the trail.

Quick, shallow switchbacks next advance the trail. Balsamroot, yarrow, Oregon grape, and low shrubs embroider the grasses. With the climb, gain views up Eagle Creek Canyon. A long, angling ascent then leads to the steep-flanked canyon of Little Boulder Creek. Here, trade up-canyon views for down-canyon ones before contouring upstream along the northern canyon slope of Little Boulder Creek.

Streams of ponderosa pine cones spill along the trail. Bluebird, grouse, deer, squirrel, and grosbeak may provide amusing interludes. Along the upper drainage, again find switchbacks through open-canopy forest. Vistas broaden with each burst of climb. In this steep landscape, washouts can steal the trail.

Contour and climb to the high-meadow and bouldery headwater bowl of Little Boulder Creek; ridge vistas pan east-southeast. Spired true fir and spruce punctuate the bowl while aspen frame the feeding springs. Lupine, phlox, and Indian paintbrush sprinkle color. Skirt a drainage of false hellebore to top a granite boulder knob, adding looks to the north and west.

In the alpine meadow, the path grows faint, requiring hikers to se-lect their own uphill line to the saddle between the drainages of Boul-der and Little Boulder creeks. Upon attaining this remote, seemingly top-of-the-world saddle post, view the ridges vanishing into Idaho and measure the contrast between the immediate snow and ice-chiseled peaks and the more arid slopes to the south and east. Winds lash the saddle, making eyes tear and adding to the wildness of the unspoiled stage.

Return as you came or proceed on the trail, descending to West Eagle Meadows and the West Eagle Creek Trail.

42   MAIN EAGLE TRAIL

Round trip: 15 miles (to Eagle Lake)
High point: 7,448 feet
Elevation change: 2,500 feet
Managed by: Eagle Cap Ranger District, Wallowa-Whitman National Forest
Maps: USFS Wallowa-Whitman National Forest, Imus Geographics Wallowa Mountains Eagle Cap Wilderness

Like many southern gateways to Eagle Cap Wilderness, Main Eagle Trail (Trail 1922, see map p. 131) presents a more open tour, with a slightly different alpine signature from the northern gateway trails. Travel along exposed rock and meadow habitats for inspired views of cliffs, peaks, hanging lake basins, and the Main Eagle drainage. Eagle Lake puts a shining crown on the tour as it glistens with blue-green clarity from its stark granite bowl.

From Medical Springs on OR 203, turn southeast on Eagle Creek Drive for Boulder Park. The route quickly changes to gravel. Drive 1.6 miles, turn left onto FR 67/Big Creek Road, and go another 13.5 miles. There, turn left on FR 77 and follow FR 77 and FR 7755 north to reach the trailhead at the end of FR 7755 in another 4 miles.

For 0.25 mile, hike an abandoned section of road, skirting an exten-sive landslide that broadened Eagle Creek's stream and flooded the forest. Where forest and meadow again interlock, find a Wallowa Mountain greeting.

Traverse a rise, overlooking the slide's boulder rubble to cross an Eagle Creek bridge at 0.75 mile. Upstream, admire a pair of broad, fast-rushing cascades. Hike parallel to the creek, passing from a Douglas-fir and Engelmann spruce forest to a corridor of deciduous shrubs. Nettles threaten the free-swinging arms of hikers who tour the shrubby gauntlet.

Upon entering the wilderness, cross small tributaries to travel the length of two narrow meadows abutting Eagle Creek. After the second Eagle Creek bridge, ford Copper Creek (3 miles). When the water is low, logs may allow a dry crossing.

Main Eagle Trail

After the crossing, the trail delivers a view of Copper Creek Falls. Locate an informal path for a brief off-trail uphill scramble to a superior falls vantage. Atop streamside rocks overlook the unruly, churning chute.

Next, pass Bench Canyon Trail (Trail 1937) and cross Bench Canyon Creek. Alders line the creeks while thickets of alder and stands of aspen mark the bouldery meadow slope. Carry plenty of water.

Pockets of subalpine fir, bracken fern, and sagebrush dot the canyon bottom as the trail grows rockier. Contouring the slope at 4.5 miles, admire Eagle Creek as it lazily slips through an attractive meadow. The enfolding high country and browsing deer may lend to the site's enchantment.

The meadow holds a trail junction (4.6 miles): the path descending right leads to Bear and Lookingglass lakes (Trail 1921); the one bearing left toward Trail Creek advances the Main Eagle Trail. As a hub for high-lake exploration, this expansive creekside meadow proves a logical base camp. Camping is not allowed within 0.25 mile of Eagle Lake, so backpackers should consider dropping their gear here. Pitch camps at the meadow fringe.

Proceed up Eagle Creek drainage (left at the junction), finding a stronger canyon impression. Along the creek flat, Indian paintbrush and mariposa lily bring a dash of delicate beauty. At 5.75 miles, slip into a high-elevation forest.

Atop a low ridge between Eagle Creek and a side drainage, view Needle Point (elevation 9,018 feet). At 6 miles, the switchbacking assault on Eagle Lake Basin begins. On the vegetated rock slope, thick shrubs produce a humid climb.

At the cairn in 0.5 mile, follow the trail branching right for Eagle Lake (Trail 1931), gathering more exciting canyon overlooks and down-canyon views with Hummingbird Mountain. The canyon offers a richly textured mosaic with spired firs, plush grasses, alder clumps, rock, and the tinsel-like stream.

A granite ridge hosts the final 0.3-mile of the climb. Reach Eagle Lake near its outlet and small dam at 7.5 miles. The high mountain bowl features steep sloping sides that defy vegetation. With minimal shade, the high elevation, and reflecting lake waters, Eagle Lake stays require sun protection.

43 VOLCANO TRAIL

Round trip: 1.5 miles (to Sawtooth Crater)
High point: 5,171 feet
Elevation change: 500 feet
Managed by: La Grande Ranger District, Wallowa-Whitman National Forest
Maps: USFS Wallowa-Whitman National Forest, Imus Geographics Wallowa Mountains Eagle Cap Wilderness

One of the few genuinely short trails in Wallowa country, this hike (Trail 1940) packs a lot of caliber for its length. The needle-softened trail travels amid open, wildflower-spangled mid-elevation forests and arid meadows. Weathered snags and stumps hint that the forest was once cut. Find ample solitude and stirring vistas upon topping the crusty black-rock ridge of Sawtooth Crater—a thick volcanic dike that curves around a gully depression. Hummingbird, bluebird, hawk, and vulture may grace a summit stay.

To reach the Volcano Trail from OR 203 in Medical Springs, head southeast on Eagle Creek Drive, which changes to gravel. Where it forks in 1.6 miles, go right on FR 70/Collins Road toward Balm Creek

Reservoir. Continue 5.2 miles to the signed trail on the left; it begins up FR 7000.740. There is ample shoulder parking near the junction of FR 70 and FR 7050.030, which heads right.

Hike the needle-coated abandoned jeep trail of FR 7000.740, touring amid immature ponderosa pine, larch, and fir. Yarrow, arnica, and wild strawberry color the grasses. The ascent is steady and mild.

At 0.1 mile, bear left off the jeep trail following a faint skid road where young larch trees have narrowed the bed. Several of the fir sport anomalous growths of thick boughs. At 0.25 mile again bear left. Small signs point out these first two turns.

In a few strides, look for the first switchback, hooking left. Isolated rocks of basalt hint at the destination. Zigzag uphill, passing from forest to open meadow along the upper slope. Here yellow bells, violets, and waterleaf decorate the way. By 0.5 mile travel below the volcanic rim, continuing to switchback, although the trail has grown faint.

At 0.6 mile, top a grassy saddle between the two raised dikes shaping the jagged ridge. A sign points left for the summit view. Hike up the crusty rise. Delicate yellow, pink, white, and violet blooms push up amid the lichen-blotched gray-black basalt. Desert parsley, phlox, shooting star, and buckwheat contribute to the show.

Glimpse the crowns of the Eagle Cap peaks, overlooking a neighboring treed rise. Views span both north and east, with Hells Canyon

Volcano Trail highpoint

135

sprawling eastward. Continue climbing to bring looks south-southeast into focus. A few ponderosa pines dot the crest.

The high point (0.75 mile) presents a full 360-degree view, adding the Elkhorns to the west and improving on the Wallowa-Eagle Cap view. Admire the open Powder River Valley to the south. The landscape is one of contrast and diversity with the bald flatland, forested ridges, and snowy high peaks. The dike of Sawtooth Crater itself commands attention.

Beware of the crater's loose rock upon descent or when making outward explorations.

44 EAST EAGLE CREEK TRAIL–EAGLE CAP HIKE

Round trip: 27.2 miles (to Eagle Cap Summit)
High point: 9,572 feet
Elevation change: 5,000 feet
Managed by: Eagle Cap Ranger District, Wallowa-Whitman National Forest
Maps: USFS Wallowa-Whitman National Forest, Imus Geographics Wallowa Mountains Eagle Cap Wilderness

This hike wraps the bounty of the Wallowas into a tidy long-distance package. Strap on the backpack for a glorious tour of forest, meadow, ridge, and high peak, with East Eagle Creek as your sterling guide. Encounter an all-star parade of Wallowa landmarks from Granite Cliff to Eagle Cap. Although most of the area's high peaks are trailless, a surprisingly easy trail tops Eagle Cap. Along the way catch glimpses of bighorn sheep and mountain goats, then revel in the accomplishment of the hike.

From OR 86 (6 miles west of Halfway, 47 miles east of Baker City) turn north on gravel FR 77; expect some washboard. Stay on FR 77 for 23 miles then turn right on FR 7745/East Eagle Road. In another 5.2 miles find horse-trailer and spill-over parking on the right. Proceed another 0.8 mile to reach East Eagle Trailhead where there is limited vehicle parking. Drive cautiously as the final 0.8 mile requires a vehicle fording of Little Kettle Creek; normal- to high-clearance is required.

For East Eagle Trail (Trail 1910), hike west on a jeep trail passing amid white fir, spruce, and huge ponderosa pines to travel the east shore of East Eagle Creek upstream. Admire the 4,000-foot vertical relief of the stark gray walls of Granite Cliff.

At 0.25 mile veer right to follow a footpath. The trail alternates between dry meadow habitats and rich woods, where firs grow 4 feet in diameter. Enter Eagle Cap Wilderness. Rocky Mountain maple, snowberry, paintbrush, and coneflower rise amid the herb-forb profusion.

The trail rolls and ascends, touring 50 feet above East Eagle Creek, one of the signature waters of the Wallowas. Intermittent tributaries mark off distance. Cross-canyon views present the wooded mantle and rocky crest of the west ridge.

At 1.25 miles traverse a rocky meadow drainage, gaining looks at "the Box" (uphill to the right), Krag Peak, and the rugged folded canyon. At 2 miles, cross the rocky bed of Curtis Creek and view a two-stage falls on East Eagle Creek.

Open, shrubby meadows now characterize the upstream tour as strong red dikes punctuate the white peaks. At 2.4 miles discover an exciting gorge on East Eagle Creek. Before long, small aspen and evergreen pockets lend shade, and Eagle Cap joins Jackson and Glacier peaks at the head of the canyon.

At 3.5 miles travel the broad meadow flat between Snow and Coon creeks to encounter the first place to camp. When bathed in moonlight, the canyon holds special appeal.

At 4.2 miles, the trail takes its first switchback. View a hanging falls on East Eagle Creek and skyline white domes, before rounding through granite outcrops and returning to meadow (5.1 miles). Talus riddles the foot of the east ridge.

Past intermittent Dodge Creek, alder thickets mark the floodplain. Cross the rocky bed of Dennis Creek (6 miles) to reach the Hidden Lakes turnoff at 6.5 miles. Continue forward, again switchbacking to travel a higher contour. Cross Knight Creek, with views up-canyon at Horton and Frazier passes.

At the 7.5-mile junction post, bear right for Horton Pass and Eagle Cap, remaining on Trail 1910. The trail narrows with a rockier footing; streams still punctuate travel. At 8.4 miles, traverse an area of avalanche-tumbled trees. A steady, moderate climb advances the tour to the canyon headwall. There find an elfin alpine forest with heather, phlox, buckwheat, and pearly everlasting. By 9.2 miles, switchback to

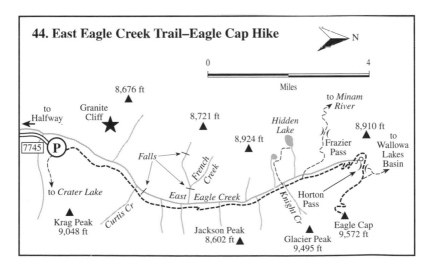

44. East Eagle Creek Trail–Eagle Cap Hike

Glacier Peak from Eagle Cap

and from East Eagle Creek; lupine and monkey flower dress the stream.

Reaching the headwall basin, cross East Eagle Creek (10.5 miles). Make a silent approach so as not to startle any elk that may be grazing on the delicate high-meadow grasses. Dippers soar the line of the creek while pikas whistle from the rocks. At this point, be sure to have enough water to complete the remaining journey to and from Eagle Cap.

Traverse granite outcrops showing pink hues, fractures, and quartz veining. Snowfields linger nearby. A consistent moderate grade leads to Horton Pass (12.1 miles). There find a cairn and commemorative plaque.

Looks northeast present the Lostine, Hurricane, and Wallowa drainages, their isolating divides, and the Matterhorn. Below, admire a cirque and a few pocked and scalloped snowfields. Clark's nutcracker and perhaps a bighorn sheep may share the view.

From the pass, two options reach Eagle Cap: The primary trail crosses over the pass, descends (often on snowfield), rounds the northern edge of a pond, and bears right up a low side-ridge at the next junction post; to the left lies Mirror Lake. Alternatively, a rocky secondary trail heads directly up the ridge to the right, starting from the cairn at Horton Pass. This shorter route generally requires no snowfield travel, and elks use it. Both summit routes merge in a short distance.

For the latter, plod up the side ridge from Horton Pass, admiring the green meadow parting the cliffs of the East Fork Lostine River Canyon. The brightness of the snow and rock makes sunglasses a necessity. Travel the backbone, meeting the primary summit trail (Trail 1805) in 0.2 mile; another snowfield typically claims the main trail prior to this junction.

Now contour the western slope below the ridge, viewing East Eagle Canyon, Brown Mountain, and Blue Lake. Soon Eagle Cap appears, presenting its imposing challenge. Reach a saddle (12.8 miles), before making a switchbacked assault on the summit (13.6 miles).

From this top-of-world vantage, find a 360-degree panorama; Seven Devils and the Elkhorns serve as east-west bookends. Relish a spectacular look at Glacier Peak, with its white cap, toothy ridge, and beautiful turquoise lake. At the base of a centrally located summit rock, find a message box. Back at Horton Pass, options for outward exploration are many.

45 MARTIN BRIDGE TRAIL

Round trip: 14 miles
High point: 3,450 feet
Elevation change: 450 feet
Managed by: Pine Ranger District, Wallowa-Whitman National Forest
Maps: USFS Wallowa-Whitman National Forest, Imus Geographics
  Wallowa Mountains Eagle Cap Wilderness

In the 1870s, Martin Bridge consisted of a toll bridge and Halfway House, providing a stage stop and overnight wayside on the Union-Cornucopia Wagon Road. This route linked the historic gold mining districts of Sparta, Sanger, and Cornucopia with the outside commerce of Union and Baker City. Today, Martin Bridge lends its name to an appealing Wild and Scenic River hike along Eagle Creek. The Martin Bridge Trail (Trail 1878) explores a "scenic" section of the creek.

A low elevation makes this Wallowa trail one of the first to open in spring. At that time, find wildly rushing, white-capped water of river-width thundering through the canyon. Late in the year, look for a quieter Eagle Creek. Pine and fir mantle the slopes; alder and willows fan the creek.

At the west edge of Richland, Oregon turn north off OR 86 at a sign for Sparta, following Sparta Road 2.3 miles to Newbridge. There continue north on FR 7735/Eagle Creek Road, which changes to dirt. Go another 7.3 miles and turn left for Eagle Forks Campground and the lower trailhead. For the upper trailhead, continue north on FR 7735 and FR 7720 and then west on FR 77; find the trailhead 11.5 miles from the campground.

For an upstream tour, start at Eagle Forks Campground, crossing a footbridge over Little Eagle Creek and ascending the campground's grassy forest slope. Pass through a gate (resecure it after passing through) to contour the canyon's east slope. Spurs angle downhill to the thin shore of Eagle Creek. Spring and summer march out blooms: peony, larkspur, lupine, arnica, avalanche lily, blue-eyed Mary, and balsamroot.

Basalt outcrops intersperse the spatially open forest as the trail travels some 60 feet above the creek. Where the creek bends, look for a milder slope grading to shore. At 0.5 mile cross Holcomb Creek (generally atop stones).

The trail rolls between shore and slope with bold rock profiles lending

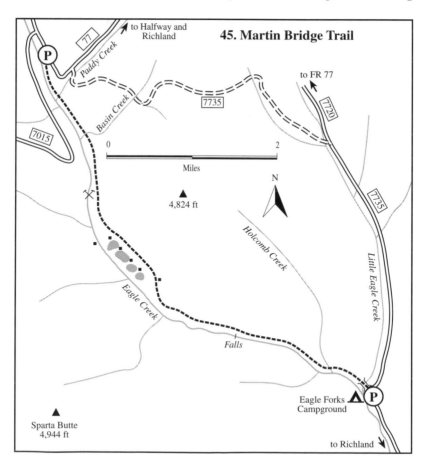

Eagle Creek

to a tour. Creek overlooks come like rapid fire. Below the rocky crests, encounter scree, rock, and often, a churning creek. The tour can be hot and exposed. At 1.8 miles view a cascade spilling with gusto. In another mile, a west-shore outcrop shapes a gorge.

By 3.25 miles, approach a handful of summer cottages along Eagle Creek. Here keep to a jeep trail and dirt road, skirting residences and private ponds; signs point the way for Martin Bridge Trail. At 4 miles, look for the trail to angle right off the jeep road prior to reaching a summer home and Eagle Creek bridge. Respect private property.

Again contour the slope, overlooking the unfettered creek. A fuller forest shades the way. At 4.6 miles, cross a side brook to traverse an open rock slope some 100 feet above Eagle Creek. Beware of unstable footing.

Keep to the upper slope at 4.8 miles, rounding above the Destiny mining claim. Be alert for this bypass as it goes unmarked and is less tracked; this is the lone place where hikers may go astray.

Hawk, kingfisher, and swallow animate the corridor and deer may even swim across Eagle Creek; each bend holds surprise. Soon, pass below dolomite pillars and cliffs. On a forested bench, downfalls sometimes obscure the trail.

At 5.75 miles cross Basin Creek, touring gravel-meadow bars, before again charging uphill. At this point, Eagle Creek presents an island-braided waterway. A little-used road travels the west shore.

Cross or ford Paddy Creek (6.5 miles) and stroll the rocky meadow shore to Martin Bridge Trailhead at 7 miles; pockets of sandy beaches invite detours.

46 CLIFF RIVER TRAIL

Round trip: 10.5 miles (to Tuck Pass)
High point: 8,000 feet
Elevation change: 1,600 feet
**Managed by: Eagle Cap Ranger District, Wallowa-Whitman National
  Forest**
**Maps: USFS Wallowa-Whitman National Forest, Imus Geographics
  Wallowa Mountains Eagle Cap Wilderness**

This vista-packed tour travels from the trailhead viewpoint, to Summit
Point Lookout Tower, and then to the skyline vantages at Nip and
Tuck passes. En route, travel Little Eagle Meadows, a captivating
cattle-grazed high range that conveys the romance and freedom of the
western frontier. Outward trail explorations may lead to Crater Lake,
Cliff Creek, Pine Lakes, and the Imnaha River. Bears frequent the
Summit Point area.

To reach Cliff River Trail from OR 86 (6 miles west of Halfway, 47
miles east of Baker City) drive north on washboard gravel FR 77 for
10.4 miles. There, turn right on FR 7715, opposite McBride Campground. Go 4.5 miles to Summit Point Trailhead at the end of the road.

Little Eagle Meadows

Hikers with high-clearance vehicles may substantially reduce forest road travel by taking FR 7710/Carson Grade off County 413, 5.2 miles north of Halfway. Follow FR 7710 for 3.1 miles, turn right on FR 77 for 0.8 mile, and follow FR 7715 to the trailhead in 4.5 miles. Views pan south-southwest.

Hike up the closed jeep road (Trail 1885) for a fairly steep climb, traversing sage-shrub slopes with huddled firs and small aspen. Lupine, aster, and skyrocket splash color across the golden and dusky landscape. Carry water.

At 0.6 mile come to a junction. Continue forward for the passes. Head right to add a 0.25-mile spur to the two-story, solar-powered Summit Point Lookout Tower (elevation 7,006 feet). (Mount at your own risk; there is a four-person maximum.) To the north, view the strong ridge line of Cornucopia Peak, with its stark rock, red dikes, and scree basins. East lies Hells Canyon, west rise the Elkhorns, and south find the green communities of Halfway and Richland. Hawks soar over the treetops.

At 1.1 miles resume the Cliff River Trail, going right. Elk tracks riddle the trail. Soon, travel the west side of the ridge, coming to a sign and the first real shade. Remain on the dusty exposed track overlooking the mottled landscape of the Eagle Creek watershed.

Veer left on a foot trail at 1.7 miles, still rounding the west slope; the forsaken jeep trail now curves to the saddle. With the ascent regain broadcast views south-southwest, with backward looks at the tower.

Atop the ridge, travel along a barbed-wire fence, passing through its gate. (Close it after passing through.) Now leisurely stroll the rolling grass-and-lupine plateau of vast Little Eagle Meadows. Again view Cornucopia Peak. At 2.7 miles, basalt cairns indicate that the trail curves right to enter Eagle Cap Wilderness. Nearby pockets of whitebark pine offer rare shade.

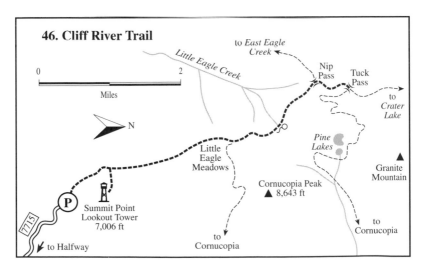

At a cattle wallow, proceed forward on the same line, heading toward the western extent of Cornucopia Ridge. False hellebore festively rims the isolated trees of Little Eagle Meadow. At 3.1 miles cross a thin ribbony stream to reach the Cornucopia Trail junction. Avoid Trail 1868 to the right; instead continue forward for Crater Lake and Nip and Tuck passes.

With each uphill push, views gain greater depth and dimension. Wildflower-dotted sandy slopes and pinched ravines mark off travel. Dizzying looks down emphasize how steep the mountain is. At 3.9 miles, cross at the astonishing spring that gives rise to full-sized Little Eagle Creek. Butterflies and Lewis monkey flower adorn this pulsating headwater.

Pass amid elfin trees and knee-high tubular plants, which are red in late summer. A picturesque basin claims the foot of the slope. At 4.7 miles, reach Nip Pass for views of Krag Peak and fellow East Eagle high rises; also glimpse Tuck Pass. Cross at the granite cairn, avoiding a trail traveling to the nose of the ridge.

Now round and ascend a talus and granite-grassland slope to reach Tuck Pass and a trail junction (5.25 miles). Here, the West Fork Pine Creek Trail (Trail 1880) hooks right, leading to Pine Lakes and Cornucopia. The Cliff River Trail travels through Tuck Pass to Crater Lake. From the pass, view the blue water of Crater Lake, Truax Mountain, Krag Peak, and the lower reaches of Granite Mountain. End at Tuck Pass or add a lake destination.

47 BLUE CREEK TRAIL

Round trip: 5 miles (to East Fork Falls)
High point: 6,100 feet
Elevation change: 1,250 feet
Managed by: Eagle Cap Ranger District, Wallowa-Whitman National Forest
Maps: USFS Wallowa-Whitman National Forest, Imus Geographics Wallowa Mountains Eagle Cap Wilderness

This upstream tour along Trail 1865 explores the steep-walled countryside of Pine and East Fork Pine creeks, coming to a day-hike ending at East Fork Falls. A switchbacking series of cascades shapes this attractive 30- to 40-foot falls. Large-diameter trees, wildflowers, wildlife, and vistas contribute to a tour. Thru-trail hikers emerge at the Imnaha River, west of the Blue Creek confluence.

From Halfway, drive north on North Main/County 413 toward Cornucopia; bear right at Jimtown to remain on County 413. Travel paved and improved-surface road, reaching Cornucopia in 10.5 miles. There turn right (north) on dirt FR 4190 to find trailhead parking on the left in 0.2 mile.

From trail parking, hike 0.3 mile north on FR 4190, coming to a trail junction. For Blue Creek Trail, go right on FR 100 for 0.25 mile, and bear right at the fork. The Pine Lakes Trail (Trail 1880) remains on FR 4190, passing through a private pack station; respect private property.

Ascend the right fork to round a gate and listen for Pine Creek in the canyon bottom. Across the canyon, view the sheer rock and scree of Cornucopia Peak. Mounded tailings (discarded rock from placer mining) echo to the late 1800s, when Cornucopia flourished as a gold mining district. The road is dusty and the grade fairly steep for the first mile. Beautiful mature fir line the route, and a passing deer may share the way.

At 0.8 mile, view the divide isolating the east and west forks of Pine Creek. Looks right find a talus slope and craggy crest. Despite the forest's fullness, the

Ground squirrel

travel corridor has an open overhead cathedral. A more comfortable grade advances the trail, as the slope to the creek becomes gentler.

Ahead, traverse a meadow slope, gaining an exceptional view of Cornucopia Peak and over-the-shoulder looks at the Pine Creek divide.

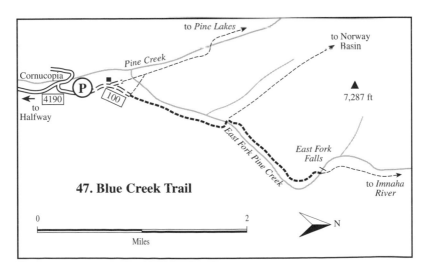

47. Blue Creek Trail

Near an enormous twin-trunked spruce, catch an open look at East Fork Pine Creek with its shrubby alder outline. At 1.5 miles, rock-hop or ford the East Fork to travel its west shore; be careful on the slippery rocks. Lewis monkey flower spot the banks and tiny islands amid the riffling creek. Dippers commonly dart past.

Fifty feet from the crossing find a trail junction: staying along the retired jeep trail leads to Norway Basin in 3 miles; for the falls hike, bear right on the foot trail. The path slices through meadow, paralleling the East Fork upstream. Indian paintbrush, skyrocket, aster, coneflower, and pearly everlasting color the tour. Springs and dispersed conifer pockets dot the otherwise dry meadow.

Past the 2-mile marker, the trail forks. Keep right, now touring above the steep-sided East Fork ravine to view a strong rim profile. The path then arcs left to rejoin the left fork (2.3 miles). Travel forest and meadow, once again viewing the basalt rim. Keep to the west shore of East Fork Pine Creek, coming to a fording just below the falls at 2.5 miles.

A secondary path ventures upstream, overlooking the rocky gorge and multi-directional falls, ending at the upper falls. Cross the creek for a better perspective on the middle part of the falls set. Monkey flower and mountain ash decorate the gorge. Turn back at the falls or go exploring.

48 SUGARLOAF TRAIL

Round trip: 4.4 miles (to Russel Mountain Lookout)
High point: 7,508 feet
Elevation change: 1,050 feet
Managed by: Eagle Cap Ranger District, Wallowa-Whitman National Forest
Maps: USFS Wallowa-Whitman National Forest, Imus Geographics Wallowa Mountains Eagle Cap Wilderness

This trail through the Twin Lakes Burn of 1994 requires some detective work to navigate as fire obscured parts of the path and stole the trail markers. Newcomers to the sport may want to avoid this hike or opt instead to hike the forest road to the tower. For the persistent though, Russel Mountain Lookout amply rewards. Revel in a 360-degree panoramic view of Twin and Fish lakes, the Imnaha Divide, the surrounding match-stick forest, areas of vibrant spruce and fir, rich meadows, an unbroken High Wallowa skyline between Mount Nebo and Cornucopia Peak, nearby Sugarloaf Mountain, and Hells Canyon–Seven Devils country. While touring the burn, be alert for falling limbs or trees; carry water.

From FR 39/Wallowa Mountain Loop Road (47.2 miles southeast of Joseph, 24 miles northeast of Halfway), turn west on FR 66/Fish Lake Road, an improved-surface road. Drive 10.7 miles to find parking and the marked Sugarloaf Trail (Trail 1887) on the right (0.4 mile past the turn-off for Twin Lakes Campground). Begin at the northwest corner of trail parking, angling left toward a log-cut passage at the edge of the forest.

Alternatively, hikers may drive or walk to the lookout via FR 450, a secondary, high-clearance route. Reach it on the right another 2.2 miles west on FR 66. Turnouts are rare on this rough 1.2-mile single-lane road to the lookout.

The Sugarloaf Trail heads west just south of Twin Lakes, which are actually a trio of ponds separated by wetland grasses and woods. Russel Mountain rears its rocky head above the basin. Angle left into the woods, and follow an old jeep trail uphill. Amid areas of burn, look for cut logs hinting at the trail. Where live trees border the route, search for the rare presence of a shaved-bark blaze.

At 0.3 mile, ascend the right edge of a meadow, again finding a section of tracked trail working its way uphill. The burn habitat holds unique discovery and renewing species: trailside at 0.5 mile, admire a 5- to 6-foot-diameter larch, a charred survivor of the fire.

Alternately travel amid live and ghost forests and across the width of long meadows. When reaching a meadow, study the opposite edge for hint of a blaze, path, trail clearing, or natural avenue between the trees. Pass directly through or at a slight angle north. Lupine and pearly ever-lasting lend familiar accents; elk sometimes mat the grasses.

At 0.8 mile, a two-track again guides travel. Grouse, woodpecker, and deer may inspire pause while live trees render prized shade. The trail soon narrows.

While making the ascent, assemble mental notes to ease the downhill return as the path is less apparent in reverse. For the most part, the trail holds a fairly steady line with only subtle shifts in direction. One such shift occurs at 1.3 miles, where the trail curves left at a sign.

Upon topping the hill, the tracked path arcs left away from the

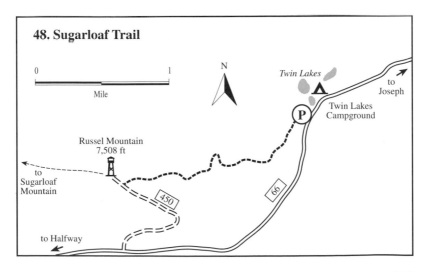

48. Sugarloaf Trail

0   1

Mile

N

Twin Lakes

to Joseph

Twin Lakes Campground

P

Russel Mountain
7,508 ft

to Sugarloaf Mountain

450

66

to Halfway

Russel Mountain Lookout

actual blazed route. Gradually ease your way right as you approach
FR 450 to find the genuine trail. Meet the road (2 miles) and turn
right, ascending 0.2 mile to the tower. But first, note for the return the
shaved blaze on a roadside tree and one across the small dry meadow
at forest's edge; these blazes point the way home.

Reach the seven-story wooden fire tower, which is ringed by live conifer and has adorning wildflowers at its base. Young trees grow
within the tower cage. Mount at your own risk, with no more than four
persons on the tower at any time. A stirring terrain radiates outward.
The Sugarloaf Trail continues to Sugarloaf Mountain for the ad-
equately prepared and skilled hiker.

49 SOUTH FORK IMNAHA RIVER TRAIL

Round trip: 11.5 miles (to Imnaha Falls, with Blue Hole detour)
High point: 5,300 feet
Elevation change: 750 feet
Managed by: Eagle Cap Ranger District, Wallowa-Whitman National
  Forest
Maps: USFS Wallowa-Whitman National Forest, Imus Geographics
  Wallowa Mountains Eagle Cap Wilderness

The South Fork Imnaha River Trail (Trail 1816) travels upstream alongside the world-class waters of the Imnaha River and its South Fork to reach the headwater basin. This tour confines its stay to the Imnaha River, visiting two spectacular sites—Blue Hole and Imnaha Falls—and passes endless unnamed gems along the Wild and Scenic Waterway. Travel an exciting, rugged canyon, passing through the mosaic of the Twin Lakes Burn.

From FR 39/Wallowa Mountain Loop Road (39 miles southeast of Joseph, 32.2 miles northeast of Halfway), turn west on paved FR 3960. Go 8.6 miles for Indian Crossing Campground and the trailhead (the final 0.3 mile is on gravel). The South Fork Imnaha River Trail travels the north bank upstream; Imnaha Crossing Trail begins across the bridge.

Hike upstream past the restroom, register, and a couple of walk-in sites, touring a forest of fir, pines, and larch. Overlook the river from some 30 feet above, admiring the captivatingly clear green waters coursing over a cobble and boulder bed. The trail then swings right

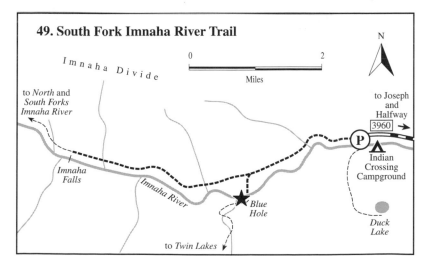

49. South Fork Imnaha River Trail

Imnaha Divide

0   2
Miles

N

to *North* and
South Forks
Imnaha River

to Joseph
and
Halfway
3960 →

Imnaha Falls

Imnaha River

P
Indian
Crossing
Campground

★ Blue
Hole

Duck
Lake

to *Twin Lakes*

coming to a T junction (0.5 mile). Go left for the trail; to the right lies a pack station.

Filtered river looks return. Find arnica, bride's bonnet, and huckleberry amid the tighter forest stands; grasses claim the open forest and burn habitat. The 1994 Twin Lakes Fire whisked through this forest at differing intensities, charring mature trees and searing younger, denser stands. At 1 mile enter Eagle Cap Wilderness.

The snag-riddled flat of the south shore sometimes hosts browsing elk, as the Imnaha waters braid and meander. Humped outcrops dot the burn canvas of the north-facing slopes. Later the trail passes amid outcrops to stroll along a gurgling tributary (1.7 miles). Just beyond, reach the Twin Lakes Trail junction and detour left 0.2 mile to visit Blue Hole.

Blue Hole features a pinched gorge and hypnotic emerald waters that are clear, deep, and teeming with wild trout. Live pines and fir, as well as blackened snags, contribute to its skyline. Scramble out onto a low rocky peninsula for an upstream look at the impressive 125-foot-long slot; a natural log jam nearly blocks its upper end. Or, top the outcrop

Blue Hole

rim for a new perspective on the pristine channel and the downstream canyon.

At 2.2 miles resume the upstream tour through a rugged canyon wild. Travel behind the Blue Hole cliffs and below a rocky peak. Pockets of live conifer, aspen, and thimbleberry dress the rock. Find talus crossings oddly free of debris.

Top a rocky pass (2.6 miles) to peer down at the Imnaha River, its deep holes, waterfalls, and swirling channels. Late-summer winds launch a flurry of fireweed seeds. Earthen trail returns as the path switchbacks to the river, rolling to and from the seductress. Spurs access outcrop promontories.

After 3.9 miles reliable tributaries mark the route as do sources of intermittent shade. View the backcountry high peaks, including Marble Mountain. More gorge-like features punctuate the river; the one at 4.6 miles rivals Blue Hole in beauty.

At 5 miles, cross a rocky high point where cliffs shield the river. At 5.25 miles, a larger side creek sometimes requires wading. Woodpeckers drill the scorched snags.

At 5.8 miles, be alert for an unmarked 200-foot side path descending through a burn to reach a low outcrop overlooking Imnaha Falls. Cross-hatched logs require high stepping. Spy a tumultuous 8-foot plunge churning through a pinched gorge to feed a narrow slot. Cupped rock collects the water into hypnotic pools. Upstream, the canyon broadens with treed flats suggesting a campsite.

 # 50 BONNY LAKES HIKE

Round trip: 7.2 miles
High point: 7,700 feet
Elevation change: 1,200 feet
Managed by: Eagle Cap Ranger District, Wallowa-Whitman National Forest
Maps: USFS Wallowa-Whitman National Forest, Imus Geographics Wallowa Mountains Eagle Cap Wilderness

This hike rounds the hillsides of Big Sheep Creek and its head forks, touring amid burn habitat, vibrant forest, lush meadows, and crusty basalt knolls. The journey's climax is the serene lake basin of lower Bonny Lakes—a large wetland water body with a meadow tapestry rim. Views include the Mount Nebo Ridge and Aneroid Mountain. Tranquility abounds when the mosquitos depart in late August.

To reach Bonny Lakes Hike from Joseph, turn east off OR 82 onto East Wallowa Avenue at the sign for Imnaha. Drive 7.9 miles and turn right on Wallowa Mountain Loop Road/FR 39. Go 12.2 miles and turn right on FR 3900.100. Follow this rough, dirt road, which is passable for passenger vehicles with good clearance, to its end in 3.1 miles. There find trailhead, turnaround, and parking.

Hike through an area of salvage logging on Trail 1819, heading up-stream from the end of the road to enter Eagle Cap Wilderness and ford Big Sheep Creek (0.1 mile). Next-generation trees rise amid the interlocking logs, grasses, and wildflowers.

Resume the trail as it slices through the bank grasses and passes amid burn to reach the north slope. At 0.2 mile lies an easy-to-miss in-tersection with an old wagon road; keep to the well-tracked path pur-suing the left bank of a side drainage upstream.

At the foot of Wing Ridge, the trail swings left; a few logs still foul footing. Young lodgepole pine and fir dot the burn, while native grasses spill at their feet. The steady, contouring ascent levels off 200 feet above Big Sheep Creek.

By 0.5 mile encounter vibrant mature fir. Upon leaving the burn, a rockier slope with sagebrush hosts travel. Across the canyon, view part of Mount Nebo Ridge, and up-canyon, spy the lower slope of Aneroid Mountain. Sage-grasslands, lodgepole pine–fir forest, and aspen vary travel.

Cross the North Fork Big Sheep Creek via stones or fording (1.1 miles). A concealed trail angles uphill to the right, 100 feet prior to the crossing. Past the crossing lies a marked junction. Avoid the trail heading right to McCully Basin (Trail 1812); keep to the path ahead, which leads to the North Fork Imnaha River and Bonny Lakes.

At 1.4 miles, an attractive cascade graces a bouldery section of Big Sheep Creek. As the slope flattens, admire the rocky ridge line. Cross a large tributary (1.6 miles) and then Middle Fork Big Sheep Creek at 1.9 miles, both of which may require wading. Broad meadows span be-tween the crossings.

Ascend amid fir-spruce forest, reaching the next junction (2.2 miles). Head right toward the East Fork Wallowa River to continue the trek to Bonny Lakes on Trail 1802. Removed from the creek, the trail contours amid forest and wildflower pockets, paralleling the Middle Fork up-stream. At 2.6 miles, cross back over the Middle Fork and resume up-stream travel.

Atop an outcrop bench, overlook a gorge-like passage; farther upstream,

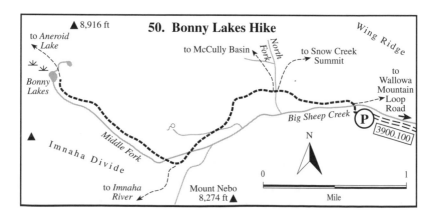

Canal Burn

view a Middle Fork falls. Dispersed volcanic outcrops and the scent of wild onions characterize the high meadows.

Next, round the foot of a low bumpy hill to tag the shore of Bonny Lake (3.6 miles)—a scenic, shallow water with Aneroid Mountain to the northwest. A textured rim of tall marsh grasses, close-cropped grasses, low shrubs, and mossy mats contributes to the soothing lake image.

The trail then brands the foot of the knoll isolating Bonny Lake from its upper companion lake. At the inlet, forgo crossing, which leads to the East Fork Wallowa River, and instead round the foot of the knoll, pursuing the inlet upstream to the upper lake for an easy cross-country, ending at 4 miles.

APPENDIX

INFORMATION SOURCES, ADDRESSES, AND PHONE NUMBERS

Council Ranger District, Payette National Forest, PO Box 567, 500 E Whitley, Council, ID 83612; (208) 253-0100

Eagle Cap Ranger District, Wallowa-Whitman National Forest, 88401 Highway 82, Enterprise, OR 97828; (541) 426-5546

Hells Canyon National Recreation Area, 2535 Riverside Drive, PO Box 699, Clarkston, WA 99403; (509) 758-0616

Hells Canyon National Recreation Area, 88401 Highway 82, Enterprise, OR 97828; (541) 426-4978

Hells Canyon National Recreation Area, PO Box 832, Riggins, ID 83549; (208) 628-3916

Hells Canyon Preservation Council, PO Box 908, Joseph, OR 97846; (541) 432-8100

La Grande Ranger District, Wallowa-Whitman National Forest, 3502 Highway 30, La Grande, OR 97850; (541) 963-7186

Pine Ranger District, Wallowa-Whitman National Forest, General Delivery, Halfway, OR 97834; (541) 742-7511

Pomeroy Ranger District, Umatilla National Forest, Route 1, Box 53-F, Pomeroy, WA 99347; (509) 843-1891

Salmon River Ranger District, Nez Perce National Forest, HC 01, Box 70, White Bird, ID 83554-9706; (208) 839-2211

Umatilla National Forest, 2517 SW Hailey, Pendleton, OR 97801; (541) 278-3716

Wallowa County Chamber of Commerce, PO Box 427, Enterprise, OR 97828; (541) 426-4622

Wallowa Lake State Park, 72214 Marina Lane, Joseph, OR 97846; (541) 432-4185

Wallowa Lake Tramway, Route 1, Box 349, Joseph, OR 97846; (541) 432-5331

Wallowa Mountains Visitor Center, 88401 Highway 82, Enterprise, OR 97828; (541) 426-5546; 24-hour visitor information: (541) 426-5591

Wallowa Valley Ranger District, 88401 Highway 82, Enterprise, OR 97828; (541) 426-4978

Wallowa-Whitman National Forest, PO Box 907, 1550 Dewey Avenue, Baker City, OR 97814; (541) 523-6391

Weiser Ranger District, Payette National Forest, 275 E 7th, Weiser, ID 83672; (208) 549-4200

INDEX

ABOUT THE AUTHORS

Over the past fifteen years, this Oregon author team—Rhonda (a writer) and George (a photographer)—has collaborated on eight outdoor guidebooks; sold hundreds of articles on nature, travel, and outdoor recreation; and participated in environmental impact studies. After kicking through leaves in the eastern United States for the past two years, they've again pointed their boots west, taking pen and camera to one of their favorite haunts—the Hells Canyon–Wallowa country of northeastern Oregon and western Idaho. With this book, they invite you to lace on your boots and discover this spectacular region for yourself.

Other Mountaineers Books titles by this team include *California State Parks: A Complete Recreation Guide* (1995) and *100 Hikes in Oregon* (1992). See also their *Hiking New York* (1996), *Hiking Southern New England* (1997), and *Hiking Pennsylvania* (1997), all with Falcon Press, Helena, Montana.

THE MOUNTAINEERS, founded in 1906, is a nonprofit outdoor activity and conservation club, whose mission is "to explore, study, preserve, and enjoy the natural beauty of the outdoors. . . . " Based in Seattle, Washington, the club is now the third-largest such organization in the United States, with 15,000 members and five branches throughout Washington State.

The Mountaineers sponsors both classes and year-round outdoor activities in the Pacific Northwest, which include hiking, mountain climbing, ski-touring, snowshoeing, bicycling, camping, kayaking and canoeing, nature study, sailing, and adventure travel. The club's conservation division supports environmental causes through educational activities, sponsoring legislation, and presenting informational programs. All club activities are led by skilled, experienced volunteers, who are dedicated to promoting safe and responsible enjoyment and preservation of the outdoors.

If you would like to participate in these organized outdoor activities or the club's programs, consider a membership in The Mountaineers. For information and an application, write or call The Mountaineers, Club Headquarters, 300 Third Avenue West, Seattle, Washington 98119; (206) 284-6310.

The Mountaineers Books, an active, nonprofit publishing program of the club, produces guidebooks, instructional texts, historical works, natural history guides, and works on environmental conservation. All books produced by The Mountaineers are aimed at fulfilling the club's mission.

Send or call for our catalog of more than 300 outdoor titles:

**The Mountaineers Books
1001 SW Klickitat Way, Suite 201
Seattle, WA 98134
1-800-553-4453 / e-mail: mbooks@mountaineers.org**

Other titles you may enjoy from Mountaineers Books:

50 HIKES IN™ OREGON'S COAST RANGE AND SISKIYOUS, Ostertag
Hikes in the mountain corridor between I-5 and Highway 101, from
½-mile walks to 47-mile backpack trips.

100 HIKES IN™ OREGON, Ostertag
Another entry in the Mountaineers' fully-detailed, best-selling 100 Hikes
In™ guide series.

BEST HIKES WITH CHILDREN IN WESTREN & CENTRAL OREGON,
Henderson
Guide to day hikes and overnighters for families, from the Mountaineers'
Best Hikes with Children series. Tips on hiking with kids, safety, and
fostering a wilderness ethic. Includes points of interest, trail descrip-
tions, information on flora and fauna, campsite locations, and maps.

HIKING OREGON'S GEOLOGY, Bishop & Allen
This guide to Oregon's most scenic and geologically interesting places
offers information to help you understand the state's geologic history.
Hikes range from strolls in urban parks to wilderness summit climbs.

DAY HIKES FROM OREGON CAMPGROUNDS, Ostertag
Selected campgrounds throughout the state which access the best hikes
and nature walks in Oregon.

EXPLORING OREGON'S WILD AREAS, 2ND EDITION: A GUIDE FOR
HIKERS, BACKPACKERS, CLIMBERS, X-C SKIERS, & PADDLERS,
Sullivan
Revised and updated guide to statewide wilderness areas, wildlife
refuges, nature preserves, and state parks.

EXPLORING THE WILD OREGON COAST, Henderson
Guide to the best hiking, canoeing, bicycling, horseback riding, and wildlife-
watching spots along the Oregon Coast.

EXPLORING IDAHO'S MOUNTAINS: A GUIDE FOR CLIMBERS,
SCRAMBLERS, AND HIKERS, Lopez
Route directions and descriptions for more than 700 summits in Idaho.

ADVENTURES IN IDAHO'S SAWTOOTH COUNTRY: 63 TRIPS FOR
HIKERS & MOUNTAIN BIKERS, Stone
Where-to's and how-to's for trails near Sun Valley, Ketchum, Hailey, and
Stanley area.

BICYCLING THE BACKROADS™ OF NORTHWEST OREGON, 2ND
EDITION, Jones & Henderson
Detailed information to cycling tours in the region, from the Mountaineers'
Bicycling the Backroads™ series.